John Gierach

Fool's Paradise

Illustrated by Glen Wolff

Simon & Schuster

New York London Toronto Sydney

SIMON & SCHUSTER
Rockefeller Center
1230 Avenue of the Americas
New York, NY 10020
Copyright © 2008 by John Gierach

First Simon & Schuster hardcover edition March 2008

SIMON & SCHUSTER and colophon are registered trademarks of Simon & Schuster,
Inc.

For information about special discounts for bulk purchases,
please contact Simon & Schuster Special Sales
at 1-800-456-6798 or business@simonandschuster.com

Designed by Karolina Harris

Manufactured in the United States of America

10   9   8   7   6   5   4   3   2   1

Library of Congress Cataloging-in-Publication Data
Gierach, John
  Fool's paradise / John Gierach.
    p. cm.
  1. Fly fishing—Anecdotes. 2. Gierach, John. I. Title.
SH456.G575 2008
799.12'4—dc22
                                    2007024651
ISBN-13: 978-0-7432-9173-6
ISBN-10:   0-7432-9173-5

Contents

You can't say enough about fishing. Though the sport of kings, it's just what the deadbeat ordered.

—THOMAS MCGUANE

Fool's Paradise

1. Trips

The truth about fishing trips is that they're often more about where you go and how you get there than about what you catch: not really about the fishing at all, in other words, although without it you wouldn't have gone in the first place. You naturally plan your trip for when you think the fishing will be at its best and try to make the most painless travel arrangements—aiming at what you hope will be a satisfying narrative arc that begins and ends in your own driveway—but the earmark of every fishing trip is still uncertainty. If it weren't, why even go?

However you travel, there are questions that go unasked because they're unanswerable but that hover there in the middle distance nonetheless. If you're driving, will your pickup break down? If not, will it make it up the last pitch on that four-wheel-drive road? If you're flying, will your flight leave on time—or at all? Will your checked gear arrive at the same place you do, and if not, will someone have a spare rod you can borrow?

The airlines say they'll deliver your luggage to you if it comes in late, but they're picturing a hotel near the airport. I still remember my relief when a guy from Air Canada finally delivered my fly rods to me in the lobby of a hotel in Halifax at two in the morning. By the end of the next day I'd have been two more flights and a boat ride away and the drama might have ended differently.

And then there's the fishing itself. Even if it's a familiar fish in a recognizable setting, there are bound to be regional quirks. On the Namekagon River in Wisconsin, the smallmouth bass were exactly where I expected them to be and they'd eat the same commercially tied deer-hair bugs I always try first, but there they were noticeably partial to the yellow-belly version instead of the otherwise identical white-bellied ones I brought from home. Fishing is full of those minute details that actually matter.

If you're after a new species of fish, you're pretty much in the dark and you only have a short time to turn on the light. A lot of being able to catch a particular kind of fish in a particular way boils down to instinct bred of familiarity, but even if you have the instinct, you're still in unfamiliar territory. (That's why it can take a second or even a third trip to really crack a fishery.) You're an adult with your head on straight and you know the drill, but some of this stuff isn't easy and you've seen people emotionally broken by a bad skunk.

And there are bound to be potential hazards that are especially dangerous because they're outside your normal day-to-day experience. They could be as big and obvious as grizzly bears, as small and neatly camouflaged as rattlesnakes, or as obscure as a regional strain of cow parsnip with sap that burns your hands when they get wet.

Or maybe it's bush flying. Small planes are more homey and comfortable than big ones (they're sort of like pickup trucks with wings), but they have worse safety records, and it's not comforting to learn that the majority of all aviation accidents are caused by simply running out of gas. A bush pilot in Alaska once said, "The only time you can have too much fuel on an airplane is when it's on fire."

Some trips are punctuated by little shocks of realization that are profoundly exotic. A friend was once fishing somewhere in Mexico, wading ankle-deep where he was safe from sharks and stingrays, when he saw a track in the mud and asked his guide what it was. The guide said, "Jaguar, señor." Things like that heighten your consciousness to the point that you're more acutely aware of your surroundings than usual. That's why your memories of a fishing trip are invariably more vivid than your memories of the same number of days at work.

Of course most of us are perfectly safe on even the most adventurous fishing trips, and statistically most accidents happen at home or while driving within twenty-five miles of your front door. It's not that your house and neighborhood are so dangerous, but they're so familiar you become complacent to the extent that you won't notice the dog's tennis ball left on the stairs or a new stop sign on the corner. Whatever else happens on a fishing trip, you pay attention.

I prefer driving to flying for reasons that will be obvious if you've been on a commercial airliner in the last few years. (Jim Harrison once said that commercial flying wouldn't be much worse if they towed you behind the plane in a gunnysack full of fish guts.) Driving gives you a feeling of self-reliance and allows time and distance to pass at a more human pace. If you're going a long way, it takes a long time—as it should—and you get to see the landscape, vegetation, wildlife and maybe even the climate gradually change. That's a romantic idea and I don't apologize for it, but there's also the practical effect that you're not jet-lagged and time-warped for your first few days of fishing.

Long drives can also make you appreciate the little things. In parts of eastern Wyoming the sight of a single tree can lift your heart, and on a rainy trip it's possible to find the almost infinite settings on your intermittent windshield wipers deeply fascinating. You're probably still on some kind of schedule when you drive, but unlike with an airline, if your partner is an hour late getting started, no one's gonna give your seats away to strangers.

If you have a moderately roomy four-wheel-drive vehicle (I drive a medium-sized, six-cylinder pickup), you can go where you have to and bring what you need—within reason on both counts. Everyone knows that having four-wheel drive doesn't mean you can't get stuck, it just means you can get stuck in more desperate situations or even wreck your car. Once, on the worst four-wheel-drive road I'll knowingly go on, I found a brand-new Jeep Wagoneer—complete with a temporary tag in the back window—abandoned with a broken axle. Years later, just past an especially gnarly spot on that same road, I followed the narrow, greasy trail from a cracked oil pan but never found the vehicle. This old logging track is my absolute benchmark for difficulty. There's a worse one nearby known as Oh-My-God Road, but I've never been on it.

As for cargo room, you can get a lot of stuff in the six-foot bed of a pickup, but remember that you'll have to paw through everything you brought once you get there and that whatever you're looking for will be on the bottom of the pile. Packing lightly is symbolic of paring away the clutter of your life at least for the duration of the trip, if not permanently, and when it's done right, it can make you feel young and nimble. For years after I left home, I didn't (that is *couldn't*) own more than would fit in whatever vehicle I was driving at the time. That lean core still exists, like a fossil obscured by more recent deposits, but I can only unearth it now when I'm packing for a fishing trip.

For that matter, if there are too many comforts you can't do without, even for a week, maybe you should just stay home, although of course definitions of *necessity* and *luxury* are entirely personal. I know people who'd never think of going anywhere without a cell phone, even though they often don't work in the rural West or far North. I don't own one myself, and when someone asks "How can I reach you?" I thoroughly enjoy saying "You can't; I'll be fishing." I'm still waiting for Americans to realize that being in constant communication is not an advantage, but a short leash. Cell phones have changed us from a nation of self-reliant pioneer types into a bunch of men standing alone in supermarkets saying "Okay, I'm in the tampon aisle, but I don't see it."

The new satellite phones are obscenely expensive, but they supposedly work anywhere. That can be handy in a dire emergency, but owning one also means there's now no place left on earth aboveground where you can hide.

I do swallow my pride and fly now and then for the same reason everyone else does: to save time. I'd actually love to drive someplace like the Northwest Territories for big grayling, but I balk at the prospect of weeks on the road for a week of fishing. So I just book a flight. My one rule for trips is: Always try to spend more time fishing than you do traveling. Still, I'm always uncomfortable flying on big airlines out of big-city airports. There are dozens of little tricks that make air travel go more smoothly, but I don't know any of them, so I invariably end up in the longest, slowest line, and when I hear one of those announcements asking you to report suspicious activity, I immediately begin to wonder if I'm acting suspiciously.

On the other hand, I have done enough flying over the years to get my packing down to a science. It's really pretty simple: you bring everything you'll need and nothing you *won't* need, while at the same time staying under the baggage weight limit. I usually check a single twenty-eight-inch canvas duffle (always with trepidation) and walk on the plane carrying a small backpack and a short rod tube that passes as my "personal item," which is normally defined as a briefcase or laptop. In a pinch, I can get all three pieces down to a total of forty pounds, which is the lowest allowable weight limit I've ever encountered on a float plane.

A friend of mine keeps detailed, permanent lists of what he packs for various kinds of trips, constantly going back to cross out things he brought but didn't use and add items that might have come in handy if he'd had them. Some of these lists have been fine-tuned for decades and, needless to say, the guy is the most efficient traveler I know. I admire that kind of thinking, but apparently I'm incapable of it. Instead, I depend on a series of mental snapshots from previous trips. I don't quite have the knack my friend has, but I do okay.

The only real glitch in my packing program came a few seasons ago when I'd seen so many people breezing through airports with wheeled bags while I lugged mine on a shoulder strap that I finally began to experience duffle envy. So I bought a wheeled duffle: a great big one that would take a three-piece, nine-foot rod tube and that was described in the catalog as "heavy duty" in every conceivable way. It was a little unwieldy, but the main problem was that it weighed fourteen pounds empty, and with my usual kit it could go slightly over the baggage weight limit of fifty pounds for a single bag. The first time I used it, a snippy guy at Denver International charged me extra for being a pound and a half over. But then on the return flight from Anchorage a nice lady said it was a little heavy but close enough and then asked me how the fishing had been.

On the next trip the bag passed muster in Denver, but at the Minneapolis airport—with still-wet waders packed inside—a friendly guy at curbside check-in hefted the bag and said, with a slight Swedish accent, "I think it's a pound or two over, but if it is, we don't want to know about it, do we?" It was good to know that you can still count on the kindness of strangers at least half the time, but in the end it was more suspense than I could stand, so at least for now I've gone back to my old bag. If you'd like to buy a large, slightly used piece of luggage, my FOR SALE sign is on the bulletin board down at the Laundromat.

I guess I've never completely understood the fisherman's compulsive urge to travel, even though I've been giving in to it for better than half a lifetime. I started young, when I was footloose and curious and when my natural agility allowed me to avoid some perils and my resilience let me recover from the rest. Also, when things went wrong, as they inevitably did, I was more likely to think it was funny or that it had some obscure significance. I don't mean in the character-building sense my father would have appreciated, but more along the lines of the bohemian goofiness I aspired to. I remember hitchhiking across the Olympic Peninsula in Washington State with a friend at age seventeen for no other reason than that neither of us had ever seen the Pacific Ocean. We camped on a lovely secluded beach and were completely freaked out when the tide came in and swamped us. It wasn't funny until we got a driftwood fire going and started to dry out, but then it was hilarious.

I still travel as much as I ever did, if not a little more, but I've noticed that where I once adored the act of traveling itself, I'm now more likely to just endure it in order to get where I'm going. I'm always delighted to finally arrive somewhere, but beforehand, in the planning stage, I can find myself as avid as ever but slightly less eager. Apparently that's not unusual because in recent years, when the question of whether or not to go on a particular trip comes up, friends my own age have begun to say things like "Well, if you don't do it now . . . ," leaving the rest to your all-too-vivid imagination.

Interestingly, I grew up with men who weren't particularly adventurous when it came to travel. They seemed perfectly happy to fish casually close to home: say, within one or two counties. They knew the water, the fish and the seasons inside out, and although they weren't what you could call fashion-plate sportsmen, they'd fish circles around the people you *could* call that. This was in the Midwest, in the heartland of the Protestant ethic, where it was considered vaguely sinful to be anything but satisfied and grateful for what was right in front of you. Down at the barbershop, you might point at the cover story in a dog-eared copy of *Field & Stream* and say "Boy, I'd like to fish *there* sometime," but it's doubtful you ever would.

Partly because of that example and partly from dumb good luck, I now live in the northern Colorado foothills, and what's right in front of me are four species of trout in several hundred miles of pretty little mountain streams and lakes. I'm satisfied and grateful for them and actually depend on their somewhat predictable circadian cycles for part of my sanity, but I travel anyway.

I like to think it's biological: some holdout from the days when we had to follow the game or starve, so that by now we have a million years' worth of genetics telling us to pack up and go, even though we no longer understand why. It's the same thing that makes caribou migrate across vast distances and mountain lions stake out territories covering a hundred square miles. Even the three horses across the county road from my place have it. They live in a lush, eighty-acre foothills pasture that's all a horse could possibly want, but they spend much of their time staring over the barbed-wire fence at the next pasture, which, as far as I can see, is exactly the same.

It was a long time ago and I don't actually remember, but I'm sure I started traveling in hopes of bigger fish because that's the usual pathology and there's nothing unique about me. Sometimes it panned out, but even when it didn't, there were new things to see and new people to meet.

I came to like bush pilots because, even though most are at least as competent as their uniformed counterparts, their lids aren't screwed on so tight. Of course lately some of them have begun to mimic that clipped airline officiousness, but the euphemisms sound hollow in the cabin of a four-seater. On a recent flight out of a salmon camp, the pilot announced that an emergency beacon would automatically deploy in the event of an "off-airport landing." A plane crash, in other words. I much preferred a pilot-comedian named Bernie I flew with years ago who said, "If we go in, tighten yer seat belt, put yer head between yer legs, and kiss yer ass goodbye." An old but effective joke.

The big bad world does try to reach its tentacles into the backcountry, and sometimes it succeeds. I remember the first time I went to a lodge where the clients were asked to sign a waver of liability (it's fairly common now). You know, "the inherent dangers of weather, boats, bush flying and grizzly bears that are beyond the control of blah blah blah . . ." I thought, So it's finally arrived, and had a brief vision of herds of lawyers coursing over the tundra in search of litigation: a much more pervasive threat than an angry bear or a blown piston at two hundred feet.

Bad timing and bad weather are the two most common problems, but in any given place there are dozens of factors beyond anyone's control that can screw the pooch, so beyond packing the right clothing, appropriate tackle and some flies that might work, it's best not to have too many expectations about a fishing trip. I know that's a big order, since you go fishing primarily to catch fish and open-mindedness is the most fragile mood known to the human race. But if you can manage it, you can appreciate almost anything that happens instead of just the one thing you were planning on. An old friend of mine always declares success on the premise that we said we were going fishing and we did. The point being, you can be happy or not, it's sort of up to you.

The same advice goes for fish size, although, again, I've chased big fish off and on for years and have caught up with them just often enough to keep me going. When I went to Labrador for the first time, it was because I wanted to see that enormous, lovely, roadless chunk of northeastern Canadian wilderness, but also because here at home a real good brook trout is twelve inches long, while up there a good one is twenty-five inches and weighs six or seven pounds.

All fishermen (and some civilians) are impressed by big fish, and when I get back from a trip that went in that direction, I always carry the snapshots around in my pickup for a month or so in case anyone asks if I've been fishing. I may know in my heart that success was due mostly to beginner's luck and good guiding, but I think it's permissible to let the photos speak for themselves.

But then the whole big-fish business can just as easily wreck a trip as make it. What if you travel a thousand miles at great expense only to catch foot-long trout, either because that's all there is or because you just can't catch any of the big ones? The usual refuge of militant

consumerism doesn't work in fishing for the simple reason that it's usually no one's fault, although that doesn't
keep some from complaining anyway. The point is, however much you spend on a fishing trip, you're not pur-
chasing fish. It's more like buying into the poker game I
used to attend before I realized that someone at my skill
level shouldn't play cards with a guy named Poker Bob.

And even if more than one big-fish trip pans out,
there's always the danger of becoming spoiled. I've seen it
happen, sometimes to people you wouldn't expect to have
that particular character flaw. For instance, a well-known
steelhead fisherman once said he'd finally lost interest in
trout altogether because "twenty inches just isn't twenty
pounds." I do some steelheading myself and I know what
he means, but I've left instructions that if I ever turn up
my nose at a twenty-inch trout, I'm to be put down like a
sick dog.

Naturally, I don't think I'm spoiled (no one ever
thinks *they're* spoiled), and I can say that, even when I
catch plenty of good-sized fish, my central visual memory
from one trip will be of a brilliant male scarlet tanager
perched on a birch twig, and from the next the poignant
sight of a crippled caribou well on its way to becoming
wolf bait. It's probably just a little extra age and my Midwestern upbringing, but I now seem happy enough to
take what I get—and you do always get something—but I
suspect it wasn't always that way. How else would I know
that it takes years to reach anything resembling a state of
grace, and that once there, you can still be evicted at any
time for bad behavior?

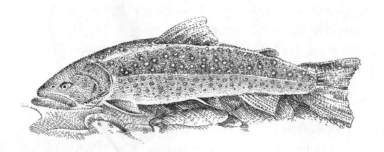

2. Bull Trout

My first glimpses of bull trout in British Columbia were like those of most other tourist fishermen: a sudden, surprising wrinkle in otherwise familiar-looking countryside. I started going to the Kootenay drainage to fish for westslope cutthroats about twenty years ago, and although I was aware that there were big bull trout in those same rivers, I was still startled to see ominously large shapes flash some of the trout I was playing and downright shook when a huge one ate a sixteen-inch cutthroat right off my leader no more than an oar's length from the boat.

The guide calmly said, "Bull trout."

I said, "Holy shit!"

Most fishermen have stories like that. Over the

years I've seen largemouth bass attack hooked bluegills, a pike grab a brook trout I was playing, a musky eat a smallmouth bass off a line and so on. It's always a total surprise, although the real surprise should be that it doesn't happen more often, since playing a smaller fish in water that holds large predators is like teasing a mountain lion with a pork chop.

I could say that was the beginning of a fascination with bull trout, but it was actually more gradual than that. I had immediately loved the westslope cutts of the region, which, on a good day and with some luck, could crack twenty inches, and I stuck with them in the same way I stuck with the big brook trout in Labrador even after seeing much larger northern pike chasing them.

On later trips to B.C. I caught some smallish bull trout while fishing for cutthroats with size 6 streamers: Woolly Buggers, Muddler Minnows and the lead-eyed marabou contraptions that came to be known as Elk River Pink Things. I'd caught small bull trout by accident here and there around the West over the years, so I didn't have to be told what they were. I also understood that at sixteen or eighteen inches they were babies.

If I remember right, I've made fourteen trips to the same area in the last two decades. During that time the number of guides on some of the rivers has gone from none to dozens and the fly shops from zero to four or five, although, amazingly, the cutthroat fishing is only slightly less magnificent now than it was twenty years ago. It was on some of those subsequent trips that I started fooling around with bull trout a little more seriously.

The cutthroat fishing was often slow in the mornings before the water warmed up, so on long floats I took to fishing for bull trout before lunch and then switching to dry flies for the afternoon rise. I used weighted Double Bunny streamers on a stubby leader and a high-density sink-tip line, sometimes swinging the streamer through a run while wading the bank, but more often casting ahead of the boat to the deepest tubs, mending line to sink the fly as we drifted down on it, then stripping it out with the halting, uneven twitches that mimic an injured bait fish.

That incorporated the sum total of what I could glean about bull trout fishing from the guides and fishermen I'd talked to: the biggest streamers you can handle, as deep as you can get 'em in the deepest water. Beyond that, just cover the river and don't expect a lot of strikes. I tied my Double Bunnies on the longest-shanked size 4 hooks I could find, but once you've seen a bull trout make off with a sixteen-inch cutthroat, you understand that you can't tie a fly that's too big to catch these things, although you can certainly tie one that's too big to cast.

I caught a few fish, including some surprisingly large cutthroats and one fat bull trout that measured twenty-six inches and probably weighed six or seven pounds— no more than a nice bull trout by local standards. The guide actually guessed it at eight or nine pounds, but I'd fished with this guy before and knew he tended to inflate fish size to pump up the clients, which I think is a forgivable bit of showmanship.

As I said, there wasn't a lot of detailed information about fishing for bull trout, and I wondered about that. If you were unaware of the sometimes complicated aesthetics of fly fishing, you might assume that fishermen would naturally go after the biggest fish in the river. Some locals do, but I think the guides rightly concluded that most of their clients would rather catch fifteen or twenty cutthroats on dry flies than dredge streamers and sink-tips all day for one or two bull trout. Also, a lot of visiting fishermen just aren't familiar with them.

Bull trout were probably never widely distributed, but it's hard to tell for sure because for years they were commonly mistaken for Dolly Vardens or Arctic char, two other members of the same family. In fact, it was only in the 1970s that the American Fisheries Society formally recognized bull trout as a separate species and not just a regional name for Dollys. According to Robert J. Behnke in *Trout and Salmon of North America*, it was at that point that the world-record Dolly Varden, weighing thirty-two pounds, abruptly became the world-record bull trout.

Like many large predators in North America, bull trout have been seriously beaten down over the years, both inadvertently and on purpose. Habitat destruction from commercial logging hasn't been kind to them and neither have dams. Bull trout have been known to make incredibly long spawning migrations (one biologist said that in that way they're like inland steelhead), and for that they need the vast lengths of undammed river systems that have become increasingly rare.

Fishing pressure has been hard on them, too. Bull trout have the habit of staging at the mouths of small streams in late summer before they run up the creeks to spawn, and when they're concentrated like that, they're easy pickings for greedy fishermen, including those who resort to the use of snagging hooks. It's probably that habit that gave them their scientific name. My Latin is more than a little rusty, but I'm pretty sure *Salvelinus confluentus* means something like "char of the confluence."

As if all that weren't enough, bull trout were also once persecuted as undesirable varmints because they ate cutthroats, so they were commonly caught and thrown on the bank to rot in large numbers. In some places there were even bounties on bull trout, but that was before both fish managers and fishermen began to ask themselves how the cutts had managed to survive in the same water with bull trout in the millennia before humans showed up. In fact, there's a good argument that the large cutthroats in parts of British Columbia are there precisely because hungry bull trout keep their numbers in check, leaving more food for the survivors.

Today you can still find bull trout in parts of five western states (Montana, Idaho, Oregon, Washington and a thin sliver of northern Nevada) as well as much of Alberta and virtually all of British Columbia. But bull trout have been declared a threatened species here in the United States. At this writing there are a few selected waters where you can fish for them on a limited basis, but for the most part, if you catch a bull trout in the United States, it had better be by accident and you had better release it.

It's more or less the same story in Alberta, where bull trout are "blue-listed"—roughly the equivalent of threatened—and you're not supposed to fish for them on purpose. But in B.C. their populations are large, healthy and widely enough distributed that, with the exception of some catch-and-release regulations and seasonal closures for spawning, you can pretty much fish for them wherever you can find them. It's probably not overstating the case much to say that if you want to fish for bull trout without too many complications or pangs of conscience, you should go to British Columbia.

On our last trip to B.C. my friends Doug Powell and Vince Zounek and I decided to pass up the larger rivers and more accessible tributaries that had begun to see some traffic, if not actual crowds, in favor of a whole third tier of headwater streams we wanted to explore. Of course none of these were exactly unfished, but some were places where guides fished alone on their rare days off and others were streams the guides *hadn't* fished but were curious about. Some of these guys were happy to have us do their scouting for them while they guided paying clients on more dependable water, so we had a four-wheel-drive rental car, a stack of maps, a compass and a longer list of spots than we'd ever have time to get to.

We were still happily fishing for cutthroats, but I'd put together a kit for bull trout in case we found some: a sink-tip line with a short fifteen-pound leader and a handful of streamers that were rough copies of a bull trout pattern a guide had given me a few years before. This guy wasn't exactly a bull trout specialist, but he was known to occasionally march intrepid clients miles up nameless, grizzly bear–infested headwater streams and come back with stories of big bull trout, at least some of which you sort of had to believe. His fly was red and black, six inches long and tied on a large stainless-steel saltwater hook. Mine were tied as copper tube flies for extra weight. I thought they'd do.

He'd also said that the best way to fish for bull

trout was to find them in the deepest pools up the smaller tributary streams where, by late summer, they were beginning to run for the fall spawn, but wouldn't yet be on the redds. Blind casting on the big rivers wasn't exactly pointless, he said, but it's hard to spot fish, and some pools are too deep to fly fish even with depth-charge-grade sink-tip lines. But in the smaller streams you can often spot pods of bull trout, creep close and sight-fish, using your big, heavy streamer as a dead-drift nymph, but adding bumps and flutters to attract attention. When I asked if the bull trout ate the streamer out of hunger or the territoriality you sometimes see in prespawning fish, he said he didn't know and it didn't matter: precisely the kind of practical answer you're likely to get from a fishing guide.

I was also told that even when you find some bull trout, you shouldn't spend a lot of time on them. Once you get off a few casts with the right depth and drift, they'll either bite or they won't, and if they won't, no amount of casting or fly changing will convince them. Better to just reel in and move on, even though the deep, aquamarine-colored pools and slots bull trout like can be few and far between.

One day we spent the better part of the morning looking for a particular stream we'd been told about, working from a topographic map and a compass and getting turned around and backtracking more than once because there were more logging roads on the ground than there were on the map. We stuck with it, though, because the guy who'd tipped us to this said that at that time of year it could be good for bull trout as well as big cutts.

By early afternoon, when we finally found the

stream, there was already a smattering of green drake mayflies on the water, and Doug and Vince immediately started catching some cutthroats on dry flies. There weren't a lot of them, but they were all big, including a couple that went over twenty inches. (On days like this you wonder where the little fish are. The answer is, they're hiding from the big ones.) I dredged my oversized streamer in the deepest holes I could find, doing a lot more walking than casting. I kept an eye out for grizzlies and also periodically blew on a tin whistle so if there was one around it would hear me coming. (Given the chance, most bears will avoid humans, but they don't like surprises.) I missed one bull trout and had another on that I lost. Then I began to get the hang of it and landed two nice ones.

I'd promised myself that if I managed to get two of them, I'd quit on general principle. Two fish suggests that you actually figured something out, but any more could seem greedy under the circumstances. I'd once talked to a bull trout biologist in Montana who described himself as someone who "lies awake at night worrying about bull trout." One of the things that worried him was that as big and tough as these things seem, and even though the name bull trout makes them sound indestructible, they don't stand up well to being caught and handled, so that hooking mortality is higher than you'd expect: further evidence that as a numbers game, catch-and-release fishing isn't always as straightforward as it seems.

Some of us eventually arrive at a concept of restraint through reason, others are shamed into it by information that's impossible to ignore, and still others just begin to notice that at the end of certain bang-up days we're not as proud of ourselves as we expected to be. In an old edition of the Alberta fishing-regulation booklet, there's a passage that says, "An ethical angler does more than what is required and less than what is allowed." That sounds all the more right for being a rare example of good, clean prose in a government publication. And then the same biologist who lies awake at night had told me that some of the bull trout I was catching in the headwaters of the Elk River in British Columbia actually migrated there all the way from Montana, where they're protected. His exact words were "They may be in Canada, but those are *our* fish." He was trying to make me feel guilty.

I'd been sight-fishing to visible fish, as instructed, but my best bull trout was one I hadn't spotted. There was a bottomless-looking bend pool along a cliff that was just what a bull trout fisherman is looking for: slower current and the only deep water for hundreds of yards in either direction. I roll-cast the streamer into the plunge at the head of the pool, mended it downstream a few times to sink the fly and began a slow, uneven retrieve.

The strike was unremarkable—just a dull, heavy thunk—and the fight was all business with short, boring runs and ponderous head-shaking. Unfortunately, I hadn't thought this through very well. I'd made the cast from the outside of the bend with fast current in front of me and a low but impassable cliff a few yards to my right, but it became obvious that to beach the fish I'd have to be downstream and on the inside. Simple enough except that to get over there I'd have to wade a steep, fast riffle with a deep slot in the middle of it. I was wading wet, in shorts, because it was a warm day, and by the time I got in thigh-deep, my legs were going numb, smaller rocks were beginning to shift under my boots and I was only one step from losing my footing in the strong current. I was deciding what to do next when Doug and Vince appeared on either side of me, grabbed me under the arms and dragged me across. Vince said, "Just hang on," although it wasn't clear whether he meant to them or to the fish. We all tea-bagged in the channel, but when they set me down on the far bank, I still had the fish on.

("Tea-bagging," of course, is when you're wading wet and go in deep enough to dunk your testicles in ice-cold stream water. It's a minor mishap resulting in nothing more than a sinking sensation and momentary shortness of breath.)

The fish turned out to be a fat bull trout a little over thirty inches long and weighing—I'll guess—somewhere in the neighborhood of ten pounds. He had characteristics in common with other members of the char family: a body that was grayish-olive overall like a mackinaw, the white-bordered fins of a brook trout, faint pink-to-orange spots like an Arctic char and just a hint of yellowish-orange on the belly that would slowly brighten over the next month or so into full orange spawning colors. And there was the diagnostic long, flat, vaguely pikelike head that marked him as a bull trout. He was more handsome than outrightly beautiful and a nice big double handful of fish.

Any bull trout you can get away with calling a ten-pounder in front of witnesses is a real nice one and well within what the fisheries types call the "typical maximum-size range." On the other hand, the bull trout guide

(I think his name was Woody) said that at a carefully un-disclosed location somewhere on this very drainage, he'd once put a client into a forty-seven-inch bull trout with an estimated weight of twenty-five pounds, but then you eventually learn to appreciate the fish in your hands at the moment without automatically comparing it to the biggest one you ever heard of. Things like fishing that are done for their own sake can seem to be about exceptional moments after which you could reasonably either "die happy"—as we used to say in the Midwest—or just rewind and start back at the beginning again. Luckily that's not a decision you have to make on the spot.

I unhooked the fish and held him in the water facing into the current to revive him. He seemed to get his strength back quickly and when I loosened my grip on the wrist above his tail, he shot off fast enough to splash water in my face. I couldn't be sure, because you never are, but I thought he'd be okay.

3. Steelhead

Every time I try on an unfamiliar kind of fishing, there's the sneaking suspicion that I won't be up to it, and sometimes I'm not. Then there are a few too many clumsy false starts, but if I stick with it, those are followed by the trip where I finally begin to get the hang of it. It's not entirely clear what the hang of it consists of, but it has something to do with getting beyond just adequately going through the motions and into a kind of effortlessness, although even that can still be far short of mastery. This naturally takes longer for some of us than for others.

I'd been steelhead fishing a few times and I'd had the kind of beginner's luck that veteran steelheaders say you can't always count on, beginning when I somehow managed to land two nice ones on the Deschutes River in Oregon the first time I ever fished for them. But then something clicked on the Salmon River in Idaho one early spring. I landed a couple of steelhead and one of them was thirty inches long, but then fish size is usually just the luck of the draw. It was more that I had my spey casting down well enough that whichever side of the river I was on and whichever way the wind was blowing, I could fish the water adequately, if not flawlessly.

At first I had to get past the unwieldiness of a fourteen-foot, two-handed rod fitted with a reel the size of a saucer. Then, given the possible combinations of current flow and wind direction, I had to learn no fewer than four different casts, or rather two casts that I could do equally well either left- or right-handed. I found it to be enough like conventional fly casting to be recognizable, but still too different to be instinctive. Chris Schrantz, who introduced me to spey casting, summed up the process succinctly. He said, "It's fun to be learning something new, but it's annoying to be a beginner again after all this time." Naturally there's a lot more to catching steelhead than casting, but, as with all fishing, step one is to get the hook in the water.

This little bit of proficiency meant a lot because I'd come to steelheading through the back door. That is, I was less interested in the fish themselves and more interested in learning how to spey-cast, which I thought was just the prettiest thing I'd ever seen on people who knew how to do it. It was only after I'd caught a few fish that I began to see what all the excitement was about. Technically a steelhead is just a rainbow trout that's born in a river and then spends most of its life at sea, but those that make it home to spawn return as deluxe, oceangoing versions of their former selves: bigger, stronger, faster, brighter and both harder and more desirable to catch.

A good steelheader is nothing if not persistent, but it's still a mystery to me how much luck is involved. It's clear that, when you get one, you think it was all skill, and when you don't, you assume it just wasn't in the cards. But there's also the suspicion that chance and proficiency inform each other—or at least meet somewhere in the middle—so that success doesn't have to depend entirely on one or the other. That's why there's virtue in simply performing the repetitive ritual properly, even though you're essentially doing the same thing over and over expecting a different result, which is one definition of *idiocy*.

By that spring I'd tied most of my own steelhead flies, and selecting which one to use was easy enough, as it tends to be. The word around the river that week was that although orange or purple flies of various sizes could work, you'd still probably be better off with the ubiquitous medium-sized, predominantly black patterns. I've heard this often enough now that soon I'll just stop asking. As someone once said, all steelheaders carry black flies for the same reason that most women have a black dress: it may not be ideal for every occasion, but it will always get you by.

This particular trip had turned into one of those mob scenes that sometimes happen in fishing. There were six fishermen (Zak and Corey, Chris and Andy, Vince and me) plus Laya and Happy Trout, Zak's Rhodesian ridgeback and Corey's chocolate Lab. There were also three

27

trucks, three trailered drift boats, three full camp kitch-
ens, half a pickup-load of firewood, an appalling amount
of gear and provisions, and a cluttered camp that strag-
gled over the formal campsite boundary into what you
could describe as urban sprawl with tents.

I never really got the full picture of it until the
morning we broke camp to leave. It quickly became clear
that whatever action we'd get would happen early (all but
one or two strikes came before eleven o'clock), so we were
getting up in the pitch dark at four, bolting breakfast and
coffee, running shuttles and getting on the water at first
light around five-thirty. But then once you're out there,
you naturally fish late just because you're out there, so
we'd pull in well after dark and turn in close to midnight.
For the better part of a week we never saw our camp in
daylight.

A party of eight—two of them four-legged—is
probably a little large for an orderly fishing trip. The ideal
group size is a leaderless partnership of two with a shelf
life of a week or so and that's often how they start, but as
word gets around, there are draftees and camp followers
like me and Vince, each one welcome but each one in-
creasing the likelihood of anarchy.

This time it went pretty smoothly. For one thing,
this was a good group—equally serious and humorous—
and although camping and shuttling the boats were com-
munal affairs, out on the water we became autonomous
two-man units that would usually pile up somewhere
along the river for lunch and a conference, but otherwise
fish by ourselves. I can only remember two moments of
real mind-stopping confusion in six days of fishing, both

in the predawn darkness, both the understandable results of a committee operating with too much excitement and too little caffeine.

As for the dogs, Trout clearly enjoyed the trip more than Laya did. Laya was a short-haired couch dog who'd never been camping or fishing before and seemed deeply puzzled by the whole affair. She didn't like to get her feet wet and got cold easily, so she often stayed in the boat when Zak and Corey stopped to fish—usually curled in a ball on the stern seat covered by a spare fleece jacket. In camp she huddled in her dog bed, which we'd dragged as close to the fire as we could without having it burst into flame. It was impossible not to pamper her a little and she appreciated the effort, but she really just wanted to go home.

Trout, on the other hand, was an entirely recognizable Labrador retriever: half aquatic, impervious to cold and a blank slate for fun, food or comfort, whichever seemed more likely at the moment—not unlike his owner, in fact. When a fish was landed, Trout liked to wade out and give it a few licks before it was released. Otherwise he'd be up on the bank rolling in dead suckers or just off exploring. He'd come when he was called, but he'd come quicker if you unwrapped a sandwich. In camp he begged handouts, smiled and wagged his tail when anyone laughed, pretending to understand the joke, and sometimes vanished into the darkness for half an hour on some cryptic dog errand. All in all, it was a pure pleasure to have dogs in camp, especially when every morning they'd go off to fish with someone else.

The word among local guides and fishermen that

week was that there were lots of steelhead in the river, but the water was running about a foot above normal for that time of year, so the fish were blasting on upstream instead of holding up the way fishermen want them to. And then with the flow a little high, there were fewer good lies and they were harder to read. But then those are always the two hardest questions in any kind of fishing: Why would the fish be in one kind of place instead of another? And where are those places?

The weather was about what you'd expect from the Rocky Mountains in springtime. It was just April, with a few pale buds on the deciduous trees and shrubs, but with snowfields still clearly visible in the not-too-distant Salmon River Range. There were odd short warm spells, but it was mostly gray and chilly with occasional rain or light, spitting snow and frosty nights. (I bundled up at night and managed to sleep warm, but there were times when I envied Zak and Corey having big, toasty dogs to cuddle with.) It was pretty much what we'd hoped for, although worse would have been better. Because of the character of the fish themselves as well as the fishermen's natural perversity, steelheaders aren't happy unless they're at least a little bit miserable and even then they'll endlessly dither about the conditions.

On my previous steelhead trips, the weather had been either too balmy or too sunny, or the water had been too low, or too warm, or maybe too high and too cold. According to those who claimed to know, it was always too much of something or not enough of something else, but some fish were usually caught anyway, and when Chris asked me what I thought of it all, I said I enjoyed the hell out of it. He said, "If you like it now, wait till you hit it right." I still like it and I'm still waiting.

All in all, it was what I'd come to expect. Conditions weren't as right as you'd like them to be, but they were still right enough that patience and perseverance might get you into a fish or two. Nine times out of ten, that's the whole deal with fishing in general and especially steelheading. People who've been at it for decades unashamedly brag about three- and four-fish days and among certain fishermen a kind of machismo develops after continued exposure to long hours, bad weather and large but scarce fish. At its worst this can develop into the belief that the only people who can catch these things are those who produce near-lethal levels of testosterone. I guess I've always been suspicious of that kind of thing, especially in this instance where, for day after day, you're casting a fly that doesn't look like anything to fish that aren't hungry and may not even be there. To my mind, that takes something far short of raw courage.

Anyway, we put in our time, worked hard, some fish were caught, and Vince and I even had a double one morning. I was just releasing a thirty-inch, A-run fish when Vince came trotting around the upstream bend with his fourteen-foot rod bent deeply and an uncharacteristically worried look on his face. I ran to the boat, grabbed the big landing net, tripped over the anchor rope and fell flat on my face in the rocks, but other than that we landed the fish pretty smoothly. It was a thirty-six-inch B-run steelhead, back to spawn for its second time after no fewer than four years at sea. It dwarfed my thirty-incher and back in camp there were the tired but inevitable jokes men make about Vince's being longer than mine.

But as with most fishing trips, and especially those for steelhead, the thrills and chills were few and far between in the context of ordinary days on the water. This was a new river for both Vince and me, but we floated the same stretch day after day because that seemed to be where the fish were, and we began to get to know it a little, including the location of some of the rocks we bumped when floating out early in the half dark. Some mornings, within the first half mile or so, a local boat would race past us bent on getting to a favorite spot first. Vince and I would always smile and wave and then make a point to remember the place the guy was in such a hurry to beat us to. In that way we located a couple of good runs that we eventually got to fish. Sometimes the guys in the other boat would wave back and sometimes they'd scowl and ignore us, but it didn't really matter. Being a noncompetitive fisherman is a small act of rebellion that often goes unnoticed.

One of the things I like about steelheading with a spey rod is that you rarely if ever fish from the boat, so as you row from one run to the next, you get to see things you'd otherwise miss. On this float there was an active great blue heron rookery in a stand of cottonwoods that we passed every morning right about first light, and we'd always eddy out for a few minutes to watch these tall, skinny birds designed specifically for wading awkwardly perched in the tops of leafless cottonwoods. Some sandhill cranes had also migrated in, and now and then you'd see one in flight, although more often you'd just hear their prehistoric clattering calls from the surrounding meadows. Sandhills, along with herons, pelicans and a few others, make it seem more plausible that birds really are what's left of the dinosaurs.

This was also one of those places where you could clearly see the entire short history of the West and maybe even a glimpse of the likely future. Many of the modest spreads in the valley had two houses: a new modular or double-wide next to what had to be the original homesteader's place, and some of those were one-room log jobs with sod roofs that looked like they'd grown out of the landscape itself, as in fact they had.

The little town we passed through on trips between our camp and the put-in was a few blocks long and no more than two stories high with many buildings separated by vacant lots. If you looked down any dirt side street, you could see clear out of town, and there were plenty of unofficial but unused spots where there was room to park a truck towing a drift boat. There was no actual fly shop, but you could find a guide if you needed one, all three gas stations sold steelhead flies, and even the teenage girl at the convenience store could give you a sketchy fishing report.

We never saw much of the interior of the place because we didn't need anything besides gas and coffee, and nearly everything was closed when we drove through anyway. Also, when you've been comfortably out in the weather for days on end, you can begin to feel snarky when you go inside, and that translates as the kind of claustrophobia that makes you want to avoid buildings of any kind.

Still, I couldn't help but notice that out in the surrounding countryside a few modern log mansions had sprouted, complete with vaulted ceilings, acres of glass and a pair of shiny new SUVs out front. A bike rider in Spandex and a jogger had been sighted, along with a gothic teenage girl with black lipstick and a nose ring. And in a burg with only one stoplight, there were two real estate offices.

Having seen the same phenomenon in Colorado, I sensed that the place was on the verge of gentrification, sort of like the Roaring Fork Valley back home twenty-five years ago, before the billionaires pushed the millionaires out of Aspen and the privileged class spread out down the river with predictable results. Once this was largely open ranch country with a few small towns where normal people could still afford to live. Now the valley is littered with tract mansions and shopping centers and modest, once-affordable houses in Basalt and Carbondale sell for seven figures.

In some ways the fishing has gone in the same direction. Once it was just Roy Palm tying flies in the old barbershop on the upstream end of Basalt: the one place everyone had to pass on their way up the Fryingpan River. Now there are more fly shops in the valley than I can keep track of, and in that weird way that upscale tourist economies violate the laws of supply and demand, the prices for everything from trout flies to guides to access to private water have skyrocketed. That's not to say that there are no blue-collar fly fishers left (if nothing else, guides and fly-shop clerks have to come from somewhere), but where the fishing was once pleasantly casual, there's now an air of competitive commerce that the old hands have more than mixed feelings about.

At the time that was happening, it seemed like the end of something, but then I felt slightly less desolate when I began to think of it as simply the beginning of something else. It's just that we all think our own golden age was better than anything that came later and of course time goes in only one direction, so you never get to point at a meadow full of browsing mule deer and say, "You know, all this was once condos."

When we met up for lunch the day Vince caught his big steelhead, the guys in the other two boats said they'd decided to do a "turn and burn": that is, get out at the first takeout instead of the second as we'd planned, hitchhike downstream to get the trucks and trailers and then do the complicated shuttle that would put all of them back in above so they could do the upper half of the same float twice in the same day. I tried to quickly calculate how many trips that would take with all three boats and came up with five, but I couldn't quite wrap my mind around the idea, so I could be wrong.

Vince and I said thanks, but we'd drift on down to fish some good-looking runs farther downriver—and also to avoid the chaos.

When we got off the water right at dark that evening, there was a woman fishing at the takeout and she asked if we'd gotten anything. Vince showed her his fish on the screen of his digital camera and she said, "Oh my goodness, that *is* big." Exactly the response you want.

While running shuttles at five o'clock the next morning, we all stopped for coffee at a convenience store in town (regular old coffee; no espressos yet), and the inevitable small crowd of old guys in coveralls asked how we were doing. I said we'd caught a few and that Vince got a pig. One man glanced out the window at my license plate, then turned to Vince and said, "Oh sure, you'd be that guy from Colorado who got the yard-long steelhead yesterday."

So it may not last forever—hardly anything does—but for now this was still a place where, in less then twelve hours, news of a big steelhead is all over town.

4. Pike

I've never considered myself to be much of a northern pike fisherman, even though I've caught them off and on for the last fifty years or so, starting as a kid in Minnesota with live minnows, then with gold and silver spoons trailing strips of Uncle Josh's pickled pork rind, and finally graduating to flies years later, once I learned that was possible.

The way I remember it, there were essentially three kinds of grown-up fishermen when I was a boy: the bass guys, the pike guys and the walleye fishermen, who were mostly dour Swedes who thought a day spent trolling was almost too much fun. Because of their relatively small size and large numbers, the pan fish (bluegills, perch, crappies and such) were seen by the adults as more groceries than game, although if you were a young enough kid with a cane pole and bobber, they might as well have been tarpon.

And then there were guys like my father, who were generalists by default. Dad was primarily a hunter who would happily fish for whatever was available at the moment, largely because there was nothing to shoot at in the summer except tin cans. He did often catch fish when I couldn't—leaving me awestruck and jealous—but at the time, I could barely tie my own shoes, let alone cast, so I could have given myself a break. It occurs to me now that I'll never really know how good a fisherman Dad was. In my receding memory he was simply the large person who seemed to know everything right up until the moment when it became obvious that he didn't: the oldest story in the book.

I remember being pretty fickle at the time, simply astonished that fish could be caught, never mind how big or what kind. I liked smallmouth bass for their strength, compactness and what I'd later come to think of as a troutlike fastidiousness. Largemouth bass were irresistible for their moody short fuses and head-shaking jumps once they were hooked. Walleyes fought lackadaisically and trolling for them involved torturous boredom, but the fish were delicious enough to make it almost worthwhile. Pike, on the other hand, were marginally dangerous, and the tackle included arcane devices like spring-loaded jaw spreaders, long-handled hook disgorgers and sawed-off baseball bats for the big ones. As a youngster, I was equally repelled and attracted by the violence of it.

It seemed like most of the serious pike fishermen I met back then were old guys with greasy caps and hands that were always scarred, calloused and often missing fingers. Whenever they caught me looking, they'd hold up the stump and say, "Big old pike bit that off." By then I had begun to realize that teasing was considered to be a form of instruction among adults, although the nature of the intended lesson could be pretty cryptic. I also knew that scaring little boys was high sport for old men and that fingers were more likely to be lost to bench saws than to fish, but I'd already been painfully bitten by small pike a few times myself, so I thought there could at least be a grain of truth to it.

I was at that eager but still tender age when I wanted to practice being like the men for a while before I actually had to become one. That seemed especially important after a helpful adult took me aside and said, "Do it all now, son, because soon enough you'll end up like me." I understood that in his case that meant having a low-paying, dead-end job, ungrateful kids, a wife he didn't like and a pint of whiskey hidden in a toolbox in the garage. Other men painted a different, sometimes rosier picture, but I knew there were hazards ahead, so I was trying to be brave and learn the ropes, wrongly assuming that this process would end with the onset of adulthood. In fact, the single greatest revelation of my life so far was that grown-ups were faking it as much as kids were. The only difference was, some of them were more convincing.

Anyway, it was obvious that a modicum of courage was expected, and of course the advice from the old guys about pike was always the same: "Don't be skittish about 'em. Go ahead and grab 'em." It sounded right, but then these guys had, you know, missing fingers and stuff. . . . The upshot is, to this day I still fish for pike from time to time and I'm still a little scared of them. When I grew up and became a catch-and-release fisherman in the interest of conservation, I began to handle caught fish gingerly so I wouldn't hurt them, but I still handle pike gingerly so they won't hurt *me*.

The last time I went fishing specifically for pike, it was more or less by accident. Ed Engle and I had gone to some lake country in the upper Midwest one spring to fish for largemouth bass, only to learn that, as you come to expect from a transitional season, the fishing conditions were blowing hot and cold. The word among local fishermen was that the water had stayed cool longer than usual that year because of a series of unseasonable cold fronts, with the result that few if any bass had been seen yet that spring, but the pike were reliably on the bite. Every fisherman knows that life gets easier to the extent that your second choice can turn out to be every bit as desirable as your first, so we became pike fishers without missing more than a beat or two.

In those weedy lakes Ed and I were fishing, switching from bass to pike was more of an emotional than a tactical adjustment, since in our experience both fish will eat the same flies fished more or less in the same way, although I know there are specialists on both sides who'd argue with that assessment. Over the last ten years or so I've gradually reduced my combined bass and pike fly selection to the bare minimum of two patterns in a couple of different colors. One is a store-bought floating deer-hair frog in either natural or psychedelic colors. The other is a long, skinny rabbit-strip streamer I tie in black, purple, chartreuse and white, red and yellow, and red and black. This is the kind of simplicity I've been aiming at in other kinds of fishing—as well as in life in general—but, for unknown reasons, haven't come close to yet.

The streamers are simple affairs with painted lead dumbbell eyes for weight and two fur-on rabbit strips glued skinside together along the hook shank. One strip is five or six inches long, the other is short, just slightly longer than the hook shank. They're tied on the style of hook known as a "stinger" with a wide gap and a slightly upturned point. A few years ago I started trimming all but a short buzz cut of fur off the strips to give the flies a long, snaky look, leaving a short tuft of long fur right at the tail that wiggles suggestively as the fly sinks on a slack leader. A bass fisherman once told me they looked just like rubber worms, which I took as the highest possible praise.

Other flies will certainly work, but those few really do seem to be all I need. There are bright patterns and drab ones; some that float and some that sink. All the rest— stealth, fly placement, depth and speed of retrieve— are up to the fisherman and his judgment of the nature of the beast and its particular mood at the moment. The only real concessions I make for pike are to use a heavy forty- or fifty-pound test monofilament shock tippet to keep from losing too many flies to the fish's sharp teeth and to make sure the long-handled pliers are handy.

We've come to think of the taller, denser common reeds as bass water and the skinnier, more widely spaced bulrushes that grow in slightly deeper water as pike habitat. We fish accordingly and it does prove out most of the time, but then we've been surprised often by catching what we'd have said were the wrong fish for the place. In the long run, which fish are biting makes a lot more difference than where or how you're fishing.

In fact, one of the biggest pike I ever caught came from what I'd thought of as beautiful bass water. Ed had been poling me around in a patch of tall bamboolike reeds punctuated by bays, channels and potholes where I'd caught several bass, including a couple of nice big ones. We'd about covered the water and I said it was time to switch off and find a new spot, but then Ed made one of those brilliant calls.

He pointed and said, "Before we do that, flip a cast up into that little pass. Sometimes a big pike will lie in a spot like that."

He was talking about a pear-shaped pothole with a two-foot-wide channel leading out to open water: the aquatic version of a game trail with good ambush sites on both sides. He poled me into range, I made the cast with the floating bass bug I'd been using, and although these things usually happen too quickly to fully register, I think I remember a telltale twitch in the weed stalks a split second before the fly went down in a theatrical splash. I instantly knew it was a pike because it was too big and too vicious for a bass.

The fish felt the hook and bored off into the thickest reeds. There was no stopping him, so I lifted the rod straight over my head to keep the line out of the stalks and felt the boat lurch as Ed dug in the pole and began to follow it. The pike corkscrewed around in there and

Ed kept us close behind him, going faster than I'd have thought you could pole a fourteen-foot aluminum john-boat in heavy cover. Neither of us said a word, which is the kind of thing that can happen with old fishing partners: the fat may be in the fire, but there's no need for discussion.

After what seemed like a long time but probably wasn't, the pike plowed himself into a mat of weeds and stopped dead—because this patch was too thick to push through, because he was too tired, or maybe a little of both. Ed poled the boat up to where my leader vanished straight down past the gunnel. I grabbed the shock tippet in my left hand and hauled up a frowning head big enough to belong to a full-grown Chesapeake Bay retriever.

I carefully reached down and plucked the fly from the pike's lip with a pair of needle-nosed pliers. He sank from sight and then swam off, ponderously shouldering aside the reeds as he went. When I looked back at Ed, he was holding his camera, and I thought, Yeah, if I hadn't been afraid to pick the thing up, we'd have had a nice hero shot.

Big fish do turn up from time to time, but for the most part these lakes aren't known as trophy water for pike. In some places the fish actually seem a little over-populated and you'll catch a lot of small ones not much more than twenty inches long. The powers that be are apparently trying to breed for better size, since the regulations say you can keep pike up to twenty-eight inches long, but anything longer than that has to be released. The rules seem to have gone over well with the locals. Most of them happily fish for keepers and bring home a stringer of them for supper most nights, but they also like to brag about the ones that were so big they had to throw 'em back.

I actually enjoy pike in the twenty-five-inch class, especially when I've been away from them for a while and am getting reacquainted. They're a good fly-rod fish at that size, with plenty of fight, and it's always fun just to see them again. These are considered by most to be small pike, but they're still a cut above the skinny, aggressive, twelve- to fourteen-inch juveniles known as "hammer handles," and you wouldn't be ashamed to bring a few home to eat. When I fished as a kid and then a young teenager, all fish were food unless they were too small to clean, but when I started releasing most of the fish I caught, I immediately fell back into the ongoing childhood project of catching things just to look at them and trying not to get bit or stung in the process. Even back then, big ones were better than little ones on general principle—whether they were fish, crawdads, frogs, bugs, snakes or turtles—but the point was more in the catching than in the size.

I also like potting around for pike in the thick tules where, whether it's mats of lush common reeds or the grassy-looking bare stems of bulrushes, a cast of any distance leaves your line draped and tangled in the stalks. The preferred technique is called "flippin'": moving slowly, staying quiet, getting as close to likely spots as you dare without scaring the fish and keeping as much line as possible out of the weeds. You can't really call it casting because you use not much more than a rod length's worth of line and leader, making a sort of high, aerial roll cast or, if you hold the fly in your line hand, something resembling a soft, lofting bow-and-arrow cast.

I like a fly rod that's long enough for the extra reach (nine feet is good, ten feet is better) with a stiff action that lets you put the wood to a fish when it runs. I'll overline the rod by a line size or two so it loads on short casts and the heavy shock tippet also helps a little, acting like a weight-forward leader and turning the fly over at the end of the flip. It may not be the prettiest way to fly-fish, but there's a gracefulness of intention and action that has its own simple charm.

It's also fun to slither a small, flat-bottomed swamp boat back into the places where solid land gives way to marsh and then to lake without any clear boundary; where it's too shallow for a V-hulled dory, too thick for a float tube and too deep and gooey to wade. This is one of those transition zones where habitat types mix, species diversity is high and a large number of transactions in the food chain take place. You'll see active yellow-headed and red-winged blackbird nests from which fledgling birds could fall into the water; crawdads, leeches, minnows and fingerling game fish, swimming snakes, frogs, tadpoles, baby muskrats, assorted smaller rodents and so on—all potential food for big fish.

Looking at the menu, you begin to understand the pike's eclectic taste and hair-trigger temperament as well as its grabbing teeth and projectile-like body designed for sudden, short bursts of speed. Survival for an opportunistic predator here depends on its ability to instantly attack and eat something that seems alive and therefore edible, even if it's never seen anything quite like it before.

Survival for the prey depends on getting enough to eat without getting eaten itself in the process, even though success for both is temporary. The food chain moves in a large, inevitable circle so that even the biggest, meanest predators finally die and are recycled by the smallest and most patient. As the poet Gary Snyder once said, without a touch of fatalism, "All of us at the table will eventually be part of the meal."

The moment-to-moment struggles in a marsh are no less titanic for going mostly unnoticed, and you can't help but think that just being alive must be worth all the trouble. If you're a bemused naturalist type, it's easy to get distracted from fishing by the details. Once on a weedy corner of Watts Lake in Nebraska, Ed and I got too close to a marsh wren nest and the adult—all of five inches long and weighing a fraction of an ounce—perched on the bow of the boat and read us the riot act. We poled away sheepishly until she stopped scolding. Another time we went to investigate a disturbance, found two large snapping turtles mating and sat there watching for twenty minutes. It was hypnotic: a cross between a horror movie, *Animal Planet* and hard porn. When we spend much time together, our conversations sometimes turn to deeply strange ideas for business ventures, so it wasn't totally out of the blue when Ed said that if we could get videotape of this, we could start a Web site called turtlesfucking.com, sell links and ad space and make a bundle.

So we caught pike off and on for several days—plus a few errant bass that were just starting to wake up and smell the coffee—but our best morning was a still, chilly one with the eight-hundred-acre lake we were on so socked in with fog that at times we couldn't see either bank. It was damp, gray and silent except for the dipping of oars, the swish of a fly rod or the muffled liquid buzz of the trolling motor as we moved from one weed bed to the next. I thought of a quote from a novel called *Rockbound* by Frank Parker Day in which a character says, "The stoutest heart is lonely on a fog-shrouded sea," but that seemed a little dramatic on a lake where ten minutes of steady rowing in almost any direction would put you on shore. It's just that when a fog finally lifts, things never seem to be exactly where I left them, leaving me with the suspicion that I was slightly lost but didn't know it.

Anyway, it was a custom-made day for pike fishing, and I got a good one right at the edge where the reeds began to give way to more widely spaced bulrushes in slightly deeper water. The fish was big enough that he'd lost the arrow straightness of a young pike, developed a prosperous gut and grown well past the length where we'd have had to put him back whether we wanted to or not. His weight felt impressive on the strike, and the fight was the usual short-range panic with line tangled six different ways in the rushes and a little hand-to-hand combat at the end.

I slipped on the woven Kevlar glove with the soft rubber pads that I'd taken to using. These gloves are designed for people who work with things like raggedly opened steel drums, and they work beautifully for pike because they're hard to bite through and the rubber gives you a surer grip on a big, slimy fish. I cradled the pike behind the gill flaps in my gloved left hand, grabbed the wrist ahead of the tail in my right and deftly lifted it so Ed could take a photo.

I have the snapshot on my desk. It's your standard grip-and-grin shot with a nice big pike held by a fisherman who's smiling confidently into the camera, just as if he knew what he was doing.

5. Creeks

While killing time in a Starbucks in Portland, Oregon, not long ago, I was idly eavesdropping on two businessmen when one—invoking the tired cliché—said that their problems might be solved if they could start thinking outside the box. The other, younger man replied, "Dude, there's no box." I caught his eye and gave him a 1960s-vintage clenched-fist salute, but he may have been too young to know what it meant. He glanced away uncomfortably, probably assuming that if he made prolonged eye contact, my next move would be to come to their table and ask for spare change.

I make a hobby of collecting found-object Zen parables, and that one struck a particular chord because

I'd been sitting there thinking about the brief and fickle high-country trout season back home in northern Colorado, which is one of the many things in both life and fishing that will never quite fit into conventional packaging. I was eager to get back to it, and I may even have been worrying about it a little, as I tend to do when I'm anywhere outside my own comfortable bioregion.

I'm talking about a handful of headwater creeks near home that flow off the Continental Divide out of two national forests and a national park, although the seasonal crowds, theme park atmosphere and the political correctness that now passes as fisheries management have put me off the park in recent years. I'm more interested in the low-rent wilderness with no so-called "facilities" and no entrance fee: "public land" in the truest sense of the term.

There are no special regulations on these streams because no one thinks they're important enough to worry about, what with their small trout and the haphazard mix of introduced species. So far, at least, most have escaped the attention of fisheries managers and conservation groups alike, which is just as well, since even with the best intentions those outfits often manage to do more harm than good. A friend once said that in this day and age every watershed should have a conservancy to look after it and that's probably true once it's attracted enough attention. But then another friend who lives about as far off the grid as possible once advised, "Just go about your business, keep your head down and your mouth shut, and maybe no one will notice you."

In anything resembling a normal year, these

streams above about 7,000 feet in elevation are only good
and fishable for a precious six weeks or so out of every
year, beginning soon after the runoff finally comes down,
the streams clear, and daytime water temperatures warm
into the mid to high forties. You expect that to happen
sometime in mid to late July or early August, but in different years it comes, goes, sputters and recurs owing to
high or low snowpacks, early or late springs, hot or cool
summers, unusually wet August monsoons, early snows
and so on. In hot, dry years I've seen the good fishing last
for over two months, which begins to seem like forever.
In unusually wet, chilly years the season can shrink to a
couple of weeks, but then the high water feeds fish and
protects them from predators, so the trout are fatter and
happier than usual in those years.

There are also daily wrinkles in the fishing caused
by air temperature, rain, wind, humidity, barometric pressure, and cloud cover, not to mention the considerable
variation in altitude on drainages that can fall thousands
of feet, through various life and climate zones, in thirty
or forty stream miles. You can fish earlier and later with
some valid hope of success and no two years are exactly
alike, but that month-and-a-half sweet spot is still about
average at the higher elevations.

In that same idealized normal year, the good fishing ends, sometimes abruptly, when the first mountain
snows chill the water again and put the fish off for another season.

Once, I was right there for the actual event. My
friend Mike Price and I had four-wheeled and then hiked
far up a stream in the second week of September. That

was a little late in the season to be fishing in the neighborhood of 9,000 feet, but the warm late-summer weather
had held in the mountains and we wanted to get high up
on the drainage one more time. It was late morning by
the time we got where we wanted to be, and although
the water was still a little chilly and the fishing was slow,
the sun warmed the stream enough by early afternoon to
bring on swarms of small caddis flies and a few flavilinea
mayflies, followed by a sparse red quill spinner fall. The
water was probably still on the chilly side, nearing what
they call the "lower avoidance level" for brook trout and
cutthroats, but for a few hours the fish fed eagerly. I always want to think they gorge in the fall because they
know hard times are coming, although what fish know is
the unsolvable mystery of the sport. Whatever, the fishing
was pretty good for a while.

Then in late afternoon—in the space of about
fifteen minutes—the sky clouded over darkly, the wind
picked up, the temperature plummeted no fewer than
twenty degrees, and it started to snow. As usual, there'd
been no warning because the front had moved in from the
west, behind the cover of the Continental Divide. It was
just a dusting at first, the kind of breezy little squall that
can come and go in minutes, but when it began to stick
on the fir and spruce boughs and showed no sign of let-
ting up, it became obvious that this would be a significant
snowfall.

The weather at altitude in the Rocky Mountains
is as squirrelly as any I've seen anywhere, but after years
of exposure you get a sense for when things are turning
for the worse. We were dressed lightly and our daypacks

were still geared for late summer, so we were only carrying light, hooded rain slickers, although at that time of
year we should have known better. Anyway, the fishing
went off and we started to get wet and cold, so we hiked
back to the end of the road where we'd left Mike's Korean
War–era Jeep.

Mike had recently dropped a new, oversized engine
into this antique for extra power, which is well and good,
except that its original small radiator overheated when it
was driven at slow speeds in low gear. It was several miles
out and we had to stop far too often to let the radiator boil
over and then slowly cool down enough for us to add can-
teens of cold creek water. This is a rough four-wheel-drive
track and the going is tedious under the best conditions.
You definitely don't want to do it in the dark or in the
snow, but of course it was getting dark and snowing harder. It was a slow, cold, slippery ride and a real adventure
toward the end, since in the gnarliest spots, when we really wanted to see what was right in front of us, the pitching
Jeep's headlights were aimed uselessly at the tops of trees.
Once we hit the paved county road, we coasted down the
canyon in neutral to keep the engine cool. Truckers used
to refer to this as "Georgia overdrive."

It warmed up a little in the days after that storm
blew through, and the streams down around 6,000 feet
fished passably well for another week or two. But Indian
summer was too brief and weak to warm the water farther up the drainage, so the high country was locked up
for another year. It was like flipping a switch, as fishermen like to say.

If I were to mark the local high-country season on

my calendar, I'd take an average and draw a line starting on August 1 and ending around September 15, but I actually do the opposite: I leave the calendar as blank as possible for that month and a half. That means no work that can't be left undone on a whim and, when at all possible, no trips away from home, resulting in excuses that must sound lame to people who don't fish. If you know how to fly-fish high mountain streams, you can almost always catch some trout through August and early September, but the really exceptional fishing—the odd times when everything that *can* come together does—can be short, sweet and unpredictable. If you let your attention wander for more than a few days, you could miss the best of it, and that knowledge makes me nervous during any daylight hours in late summer when I'm not on the water.

Obviously this has all come to seem real important, as if it were part of a private religion observed by spending weeks at a time living a parody of a nineteenth-century life in the twenty-first century. This tendency goes back at least as far as my early teens. I can remember my father introducing me at the time as his son who was "born a hundred years too late," which I took as a compliment. If nothing else, it was better than his previous explanation that I was so unlike the rest of the family because I'd been left on the doorstep by Gypsies.

You naturally think that with most of your adult life spent on the same water you should be able to predict the best fishing, and God knows I've tried. After all, we Americans have convinced ourselves that you can't be said to understand something unless you can accurately predict it, whether it's the weather, the stock market or trout fishing. Most of what I know about these creeks has sunk in subliminally over time and now feels instinctive, but I've kept a journal that I now and then actually consult, and during a quasi-scientific stage I did some fairly serious reading, including a paper with the daunting phrase "altitudinal zonation" in its title. I learned several interesting things I didn't already know, filled in some historical gaps and had a few sneaking suspicions confirmed, but none of it helped my powers of prediction all that much. That is, everything that happens is entirely familiar, but I don't always see it coming.

It's true that after years of exposure, if not actual study, you can develop a nose for what constitutes a perfect storm of conditions at any given altitude, but it also helps to spend many days on the water to increase your odds. Even then you're often left to figure out in hindsight why the fishing was so much better one day than another.

I naturally brag to friends after the best trips, but in that sense I'm like a kid who throws twenty-eight rocks at a tin can, hits it five times and later just says, "I hit it five times!" Even when I've managed to convince myself that I have these creeks wired, I sometimes idly wonder how I'd do if I just flipped a coin to see when I'd go fishing and then tossed a dart at a map to decide where.

But my usual M.O. is to fish hard until I hit the so-far-inevitable few days when the fishing itself and the size of the trout are both close to what I selectively remember from twenty or thirty years ago. I don't quit there by any means, although it has occurred to me recently that I could, since this is just a way of celebrating a kind of perfection in the face of all the evidence to the contrary. I don't have any illusions about permanence, nor do I necessarily fear change except that it's so seldom for the better. It's just that I can live with any number of things going straight to hell as long as these streams continue to hold up. If this amounts to living in a fool's paradise, don't waste your time trying to explain that to the fool.

The first time I caught it right this season was in early August on a creek I know in a neighboring county: a roadside stretch in the neighborhood of 7,500 feet. It does get some casual fishing pressure near the turnouts, but there are a few steep, boulder-strewn, overgrown sections that are so hard to get around in that they're still almost untouched. In one way, these streams are fluid, continuous ecosystems, but in another way they amount to chains of distinct microhabitats, so the fishing can improve tremendously in no more than a few hundred yards of undisturbed water.

There were no real heroics to the fishing that day unless you count the god-awful bushwhacking and rock scrambling or the black bear I surprised at a range of about twenty yards. I'd been picking my way slowly upstream with my head down to watch where I was putting my feet. He'd apparently been getting a drink from the creek because when I looked up and saw him staring at me, there was water dripping from his chin. I told him he was a good bear and a pretty bear in the voice I've heard horsemen use to calm nervous mounts, and clumsily backed into what, up to that moment, I'd considered to be an impenetrable patch of water birch on my side of the stream, losing my straw hat in the process. When I peeked a few minutes later, he was gone, so I retrieved my hat and kept fishing.

The water temperature and stream flow were both close to perfect that day and there were plenty of bugs on the water, mostly caddis flies, yellow sallies, and red quills. It was a hot, bright August afternoon and the high-altitude sunlight had warmed the water nicely, but the steep canyon wall shaded the stream by midafternoon, so the brown trout that can be so shy in direct light were looking up and eager to rise.

Not counting the usual casting and wading difficulties, the fishing was fairly easy. I cherry-picked the water, casting only to the deepest, fishiest-looking plunge pools, caught nine chubby brown trout between eleven and thirteen inches and missed maybe five others of roughly the same size. I'd tied on a Red Quill variation of mine that's named for that stream, but in retrospect I think it was one of those days when any fly in size 14 or 16 that floated would have done the trick.

I *have* tied a few fly patterns intended especially for these creeks, but that says more about fly tiers being incurable tinkerers than it does about the fishing. To prove just that point, Mike Price once spent most of a season fishing entirely with Royal Coachmen and Gray Hackle Peacocks and catching at least as many fish as anyone else. He chose those particular outdated patterns because they were the same ones he used nearly fifty years ago when he started fishing these streams as a "redneck kid" (his words).

On the way out that day, I got above the narrow band of thick bankside birch and willow and picked my way along the more open side of the slope. This is mostly slanted granite bedrock covered with loose gravel, and as a surface to walk on it's like a tile floor tilted at an angle and sprinkled with ball bearings. In years past I've put dings in the reel seats of two bamboo fly rods and pale scars on my bare knees and elbows doing this, but it seems necessary. It would have been easier and safer to simply climb another forty feet up to the road and walk back along the shoulder, but I didn't want anyone to see me there with a fly rod for fear that they'd start to get ideas.

You do end up with favorite, dependable spots on your home water that you want to keep to yourself, even if, as time goes by, that begins to look like a losing battle. The best are the overlooked places you located by being cagey (by either going farther than everyone else or by stopping sooner), although most are just the results of good old trial and error. You start with the assumption that any trout stream, from the best to the most ordinary, has more to offer than is immediately evident. Then you go on from there—sometimes for decades.

You also learn to recognize the quality of the gift. In this case, with only a handful of exceptions over the last thirty-some years, trout between eleven and thirteen inches are about the best these streams have to offer—and only a damned fool would turn up his nose at the best of anything. I've been told by some that in the grand scheme of fly fishing, trout of that size are a pretty low benchmark to set for yourself. Maybe I'm missing something, but that strikes me as an advantage.

I've also talked to fishermen who say they're disappointed in these creeks. They say they fished them once or twice (usually in the easiest, most obvious places) and only caught dinks. A few of them sounded vaguely accusatory. They seemed to be wondering if I'm exaggerating the size of trout I say I sometimes manage to catch, or if maybe I'm living hopelessly in the past when, as everyone knows, all fish were bigger. But when one guy said recently "I must not be fishing where you are," I thought, Yeah, let's hope not, and left it at that. Anyone who wants to walk away from these creeks thinking they're not good enough has my blessing.

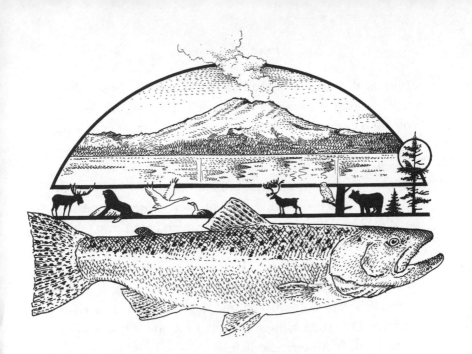

6. Volcano

I'd been home from a successful salmon fishing trip to Alaska for about three weeks when Ed Engle called. He skipped the small talk and said that the fish we'd caught there were virtually the last ones seen in the river, even though we'd been fishing at what was supposed to have been the very beginning of the run. He said the entire season was in the process of going right in the toilet and it wasn't exactly clear why, but added, "They're saying it has something to do with the volcano." This is the kind of call you'll get the minute you think you've just about heard it all.

Sometime later, Jon Kent, the owner of the camp where we'd stayed, sent a letter filling in more of the story.

Chiginagak Volcano at the headwaters of the King Salmon River had experienced what scientists at the Alaska Volcano Observatory were calling an "event." There was no eruption, but rapid heating in the crater had abruptly melted the mountain's glacier and the snowcap on its 7,000-foot summit, sending a flood of sulfury "toxic slurry" into Mother Goose Lake that then gradually percolated on down the river. We hadn't noticed anything while we were there, even though, by all accounts, the event had begun a few weeks earlier. But within a week or so after we left, the river started to smell like rotten eggs, globs of reddish-yellow foam began to appear, and in a river renowned for runs of five species of salmon, plus sea-run Arctic char, there were no fish.

Jon said the king and chum salmon we caught were those heading to spawn in a pair of tributary creeks that entered the river within a mile or two of the ocean. The streams' combined flows produced a plume of unpolluted water the fish could follow along one bank from the Bering Sea, while the bulk of the fish going up the main current to spawn upriver, guided by scent, got a whiff of sulfur and simply turned around and went back to sea.

Jon said there was no evidence of a fish kill and that the smolts (the young salmon that stay in the river for a year or two before migrating to the ocean) were clustered in the clean water around the mouths of tributaries, where they'd likely survive. Many of the river's waterbirds left, too, much of the bankside vegetation was dying off, and although we saw three brown bears while we were there, they and the ones that arrived later would have wandered off when the usual summer-long feast of salmon didn't materialize. Naturally, Jon called his clients and canceled the season as soon as it became obvious what was happening.

I was worried about Jon, who depends on the salmon runs for his living, and of course I had immediately come to love this river in the same way I love all the rivers I fish, or *have* fished or might yet fish if I live long enough—that is, more than just theoretically owing to my own self-interest. Otherwise this could have been nothing more than an interesting natural history lesson, another example of the world we live in doing what it does without regard for our convenience or livelihood. On the other hand, an entire wilderness salmon river emptied of fish by a volcano struck me as a little too biblical to fall under the easy heading of "shit happens."

But then I also understood that at a certain point in late middle age a cup of coffee that's gone cold can get you contemplating mortality and that we spend entirely too much time wondering how we "feel" about things when, in most cases, how we feel couldn't matter less. As the Buddha said, "Life sucks; get over it," or words to that effect.

A little less than a month earlier I'd met up with Ed at a hotel in Anchorage, where we managed a scant few hours' sleep before heading back to the airport. (If I had it to do over again, I'd doze in a chair somewhere and save the price of the room.) The next morning at the gate for our PenAir flight, I met Ed's friend Sam Haddon, a federal district court judge from Montana. Ed had predicted that

Sam and I would disagree politically, but that we'd like each other anyway, which is exactly how it turned out, mostly because Sam owned the specific talent of being able to remove his judicial robe to reveal the regular old fisherman underneath.

The three of us would be the only ones fishing out of the lodge, but then it was a week before the place officially opened and we were ostensibly there to help scout the beginning of the king salmon run with Jon and his guides. (This was an obvious pretext, since the last thing these guys needed when it came to salmon fishing was our help.) Anyway, Ed and Sam were regulars with several trips to this lodge under their belts. I was the newcomer, there because Jon had invited me and because Ed, my oldest and most trusted fishing friend, told me I should go.

From Anchorage we flew down the Alaskan Peninsula to the settlement of King Salmon, where the one-room terminal was crowded with sport and commercial fishermen, petroleum industry types and a few others who were harder to pigeonhole. But even if you couldn't guess what everyone was up to, you could spot those returning to civilization because their faces and body language registered the full gamut of emotions from satisfaction to disappointment to the plain physical weariness of those who—like me—don't sleep well in a place where it doesn't get dark at night.

In remote airports like this, everyone seems to understand—either through instinct or experience—that they are out on the ragged edge of commercial aviation where itineraries fall somewhere between suggestions and educated guesses, so they each exhibit their own version of forbearance. Once they're out of cell phone range, even the most obvious type-A travelers begin to experience a kind of numb acceptance, and to further make the point some backcountry aviators wear baseball caps that read I DON'T KNOW WHEN THE PLANE WILL GET HERE.

I settled in with a good book (*Spartina* by John Casey), reminding myself that the happiest pilgrims are those who have mastered patience and that in the years I've been traveling in the far north, I'd always eventually reached my destination and the latest I'd ever been was a mere two days. Also that on every trip there's a moment when you realize you're not where you're going yet, but you are definitely someplace else, and this was it.

But then after only a three-hour wait and some day-old, free coffee, a young bush pilot ambled over and asked if we were the guys going to Pumice Creek.

I said, "Actually, it's *Painter* Creek."

He said, "Okay, sure, we can do that," and we followed him out onto the landing strip toward a trim little green and white Cessna Caravan.

These flights can easily turn into endless milk runs, but this time there was only one quick stop at Pilot Point to deliver mail and pick up a six or seven-year-old Athabascan girl who was traveling alone to see relatives. She hugged her nondescript stuffed animal with hands calloused from pulling nets and announced that she was a salmon fisherman, too—one of the best, in fact. We didn't doubt it.

It was a clear day, and from the air the lodge at Painter Creek looked fragile and insignificant, as all remote fishing camps do. There was a simple frame lodge, some scattered outbuildings, cabins for the sports, and a few downright primitive hooches for the guides, all set on a rise above the creek away from the worst of the mosquitoes. The dirt airstrip cut into a grove of black cottonwoods was adequate without being what you could call plumb level or arrow straight.

The camp sits in the foothills of the short King Salmon River drainage, no more than thirty miles from Ugashik Bay on the Bering Sea. From the narrow porch of the lodge you can see Mother Goose Lake in the distance—the headwaters of the river—and on a clear day the snowcapped but still-active Chiginagak Volcano along the spine of the Aleutian Range. Some days the plume of steam from its vent looks like a horizontal mare's tail cloud, other days it's more like smoke rising from a campfire. The sight seems slightly ominous at first, but you get used to it.

Later in the season you can fish much closer to camp—in the upper river or in Painter Creek itself—but the program for the first of the kings is to jet-boat miles downriver to the sub-Arctic coastal plain within a few miles of the ocean, where the fish could begin to come in on any high tide.

You know the procedure for scouting: You spread out along a likely-looking bank and blind-cast systematically for an hour or so to thoroughly work the water. When it doesn't pan out, the guide whistles you back to the boat and you motor off in a businesslike way to try another spot. Impatience is futile. The fish are where they are—wherever that is—and in the peculiar perspective of a fishing trip, it's still early and you have what amounts to all the time in the world.

As it turned out, we spent the better part of two days going from one good channel to another looking for salmon and not finding them. The weather was mostly sunny with temperatures in the seventies and Ed thought maybe that was putting the fish off. I thought it was timing. Hitting a run of anadromous fish is tricky at best, and even if we were right on the money, the salmon would only be starting to nose into the river. Jon and the guides nodded noncommittally at both theories but said the fish should be in and you'd expect to see a few, even if you couldn't catch them. They seemed a little puzzled, although I don't think they were worried yet. Then again, the best guides rarely fret in front of their clients.

I've never met an experienced angler who minds a slow start to a fishing trip, and some of us have even come to prefer it. A gradual beginning builds the proper amount of drama for any successes that are yet to come and also allows you to settle into a sustainable routine, as opposed to going like hell for a few days and then hitting a wall of exhaustion. It also gives you the leisure to identify the most obvious birds (red-throated loons, snowy owls, tundra swans), to see some otters, moose, caribou, brown bears, and maybe the odd Alaska fur seal, and generally to soak up the open, empty wind-blown landscape. Once the fishing gets hot and heavy, a profound silence is broken by splashing and yelling, and a lot of wildlife and scenery that you may never see again dissolves in the commotion. You're on a lovely, remote wilderness river in the Alaskan backcountry. There are people who would make this trip and not even bring a fishing rod.

Paul Tickner, the guide Ed and I spent the most time with, was a perfect match for us because he's as avid a wildlife watcher as we are—so much so that he always arranged to be the first boat downriver in the morning and the first back up in the evening. That's because the first boat sees all the critters, but also scares many of them away for the second boat.

Every day, regardless of whatever else we happened to see, there was a quick stop at an active bald eagle nest (quick because if you lingered too long, one of the adults would dive at you) and a visit to a pair of great horned owls with some young that had just left the nest to teeter in the nearby cottonwood limbs. The adult owls are handsome, dignified creatures, but the owlets look like something a teddy bear designer might dream up after a weeklong binge. Paul naturally knew all the birdcalls, but said his favorite was the sad little song of the golden-crowned sparrow that sounds like the first three notes of "Three Blind Mice" whistled in a minor key.

On the third day we finally located some king salmon in a channel below a tributary creek. There was a wide, shelving riffle, and the fish were loosely stacked in the long run below it, waiting for the river to rise with the next high tide. By then a front had moved in and the weather had turned chilly and overcast with a stiff breeze and intermittent spitting rain—more like what you expect from coastal Alaska and better weather for salmon fishing. The fish were mostly invisible in the flat, gray light, but now and then one would ghost up the near bank or roll lazily out in the main current.

Even when you know the fish are there, the drill is the same as it is for scouting: You cover the water by making your longest possible cast with a high-density sink-tip line and swinging your fly across and downstream. After a few casts you take several steps downstream and do it again, and so on, painting the river with three- or four-foot-wide stripes so that every fish you can reach has a chance to see the fly. The tackle is stout: a ten-weight rod, a twenty-pound test leader and flies tied on size 2/0 to 4/0 salmon hooks. Everyone's first color choice is hot pink with some silver tinsel. If that fails, try purple and black. They say you can carry more flies if that makes you feel better, but those two are all you really need.

My first few fish were jacks—immature, three- or four-pound king salmon that run upriver with the adults—and then I hooked a much heavier fish that ran me far downstream, followed by Paul with his long-handled landing net. It turned out to be a bright salmon weighing a little over twenty pounds. Ed knew I'd never fished for kings before, so once the required snapshot was taken and the fish was released, he grinned and said he'd been hoping I'd get into some of those "middle-sized ones."

Middle-sized ones? I took a minute to adjust my sense of scale and for some reason flashed back to 1959, when Alaska gained statehood, suddenly making Texas the *second*-largest state in the Union. Among the jokes that went around then was the one about the conceited Texan who visits his friend in Alaska. They're in a hardware store in Anchorage when the Texan stops at what he assumes is a roll of chicken wire and says, "Hell, the chickens back home would walk right through that." The Alaskan replies, "That ain't chicken wire; it's mosquito netting."

During the next half hour of methodical casting, I wondered how it was that I could remember a joke from 1959 but not what I had for breakfast that morning.

For the next few days we caught kings up and down that channel weighing between fifteen and twenty-five pounds, plus some hot chum salmon up to ten and twelve pounds from the faster water upstream. The kings (called chinooks outside Alaska) were thick, but streamlined with tails like shovels and the general heft of a pine log. They're silvery when they first come in from the ocean for the spawning run, but once in fresh water they quickly turn pink, then rose, then dark red. Some think they're prettier when they're colored up—even though that's a sign of the decomposition that will eventually kill them—but fishermen like the silver or "bright" fish because they're fresh from the salt and at their strongest.

The kings were the biggest, handsomest fish and definitely the main event, but I also liked the chums (a.k.a. dog salmon) for their unlikely hideousness. They're shorter, deeper in the body and more compact than other salmon, with humped backs and, on the spawning males, long faces with grotesquely kyped jaws full of large, crooked teeth. Once they're in fresh water, their oceangoing chrome bodies darken to a calico pattern of sickly greens, purples and dark reds. For all Pacific salmon, the spawning run is a death sentence and, more than any other species, chums look like they must feel.

My biggest king was a bright hen that weighed slightly over thirty pounds and was probably fresh from the ocean on the last tide. I hooked her late in the trip when I had some idea of what to expect, but I still spent fifteen minutes running up and down the bank, trying not to step in a beaver hole and break my leg and otherwise doing whatever those of us who don't pray do instead. Paul, sensing the onset of panic, ambled over and coached me through it in the kind of pointedly calm voice you'd use on a frightened child or a cornered homicidal maniac.

In the grand scheme of things, thirty pounds is not all that large for a king salmon, although on that particular river it's considered to be on either the low end of big or the high end of middle-sized, worthy of more than just polite excitement from guides and partners. Whatever, it was the biggest fish I'd ever caught, and once I'd finally turned her big head downstream into the net, my legs went all rubbery, I couldn't quite catch my breath and when I raised the fish toward the waiting camera, it seemed almost too heavy to lift. Ed said, "Smile," and as the shutter clicked, I said, "Huh?" When I show the photo to people now, they say, "Nice fish, but what's with the look on your face?"

As it turned out, we caught all our salmon in that one long stretch below those tributary creeks, and although we dutifully scouted other spots every day, we never did find any more. Jon said the fishing had been slow in terms of the usual excess that lures many fishermen to Alaska, but Ed, Sam, and I had all landed what seemed to us to be plenty of big fish and were happy in the myopic way of visiting fishermen. But the guides were now openly concerned by the absence of salmon in the rest of the lower river. Even if the run was a little late, they said, the place should have been starting to fill with kings.

Meanwhile, the season was just beginning and fishermen with high expectations had already bought plane tickets.

That's how we left it when we flew out at the end of the week: as the kind of fully resolved narrative that you can—and usually do—begin telling as soon as you get home. The return trip was uneventful except for a stop on the way back to King Salmon when we landed on the beach at the fishing village of Egegik to pick up a load of salmon roe bound for Japan. The place was badly socked in with fog, but the pilot made a pass at the beach anyway. (You do this to get your bearings and also to warn people on the ground to get out of the way. Then you circle around and set it down.) I couldn't make out the beach below us on the first pass, but I knew we were damned close because the fog was filled with the gray and white backs of a thousand herring gulls we'd flushed. It was one of the most eerily beautiful things I've ever seen, and at the same time I wondered, Is being in this little airplane at this moment that fatally stupid thing I've been trying so hard not to do?

Later the pilot said you can safely fly low there because the tallest thing within miles is a flagpole on a one-story building. "There was absolutely no danger," he added.

I got the news of the volcano from Ed a few weeks later, then the letter from Jon arrived, and then I ran into Paul at a sportsman's show in Denver, where he told me he'd picked up a job guiding for steelhead on Kodiak Island. I didn't talk to Jon again until September of the following year and then only briefly because he was speaking from the lodge on an exorbitantly expensive satellite phone. The upshot was that the fish had begun to return, even though the river hadn't yet flushed itself to the point that the water chemistry was completely back to normal. (It's possible that these fish have grown used to the lingering aroma of the volcano and that a hint of brimstone might even be part of the olfactory signature of their home water.) Not knowing what to expect, Jon hadn't booked clients for that year, but he did have two fishermen who knew the score in for king season. Early in the conversation he said they landed over a hundred salmon in six days. Later he bumped the figure to a hundred and twenty.

The silver salmon came in later, more or less on schedule, and Jon said that just that day he'd taken a boat upstream to pick up some moose hunters and seen schools of sea-run char and chum salmon in Painter Creek. The tentative plan was to begin to bring fishermen in on a limited basis the following year with the option of fly-outs to other rivers nearby, just in case.

The lodge had also hosted a team of volcanologists from the university that summer who said, matter-of-factly, that Chiginagak is a young volcano barely half a million years old and still suffering from growing pains. Apparently you can expect little burps like this—not quite predictably—every thirty years or so, and a full-blown eruption isn't entirely out of the question. Jon also talked to an old guide who had worked the river thirty years ago when, sure enough, a similar event had occurred. The man said that after two years all the runs were back to normal and with two extra seasons feeding in salt water, the fish were bigger.

On the phone Jon sounded typically boisterous, relieved and also oddly rested for a lodge owner. He said he and his wife, Patty, had spent most of the summer scouting the river, painting the lodge, cutting and stacking firewood, having some friends up to visit and grilling and eating salmon. I got the impression that after decades of wrangling fishermen, with their myriad expectations, quirks and inadequacies, it hadn't been all bad.

I didn't ask because it was none of my business, but the lost season must have been a hard financial hit, not unlike a farmer losing a crop, which, depending on how things stand, can be anywhere from the final nail in the coffin to just something that was bound to happen eventually. Few fishing lodges operate very far into the black even when things are going perfectly, and several outfitters I know have admitted that their "business plan" simply amounts to living the life without going broke.

For my part, I had scrupulously avoided "getting in touch with my feelings" about all this, but it had still gradually evolved from the worst fishing horror story I'd ever heard with the happiest probable ending to a lesson in impermanence, to the ultimate in fisherman's luck, since in an entire season there was that one week of good fishing and I'd been there for it. What are the odds of that?

7. Road Books

I was looking over some literature for a fishing camp in Canada when it occurred to me that these brochures are a little like contracts. That is, one tends to be pretty much like another, but somewhere in what amounts to the small print is the catch you're looking for.

In this one there was the usual boilerplate about the big fish, great food, soft beds and skilled guides (which is true more often than not) as well as the regulation paragraph about how the weather there "must be respected and planned for properly." This brochure went on to suggest that you bring the usual warm clothing that can be worn in layers and that will dry out easily, as well as some good rain gear: fair advice for any fishing trip. There were also two references to mosquito repellent, the second in italics.

But the most revealing hint about the conditions was that along with all your other gear, you should bring "a couple of good books." Not just a good book, mind you, but a couple of them, because apparently it's not that unusual to be stuck in this camp through more than one fat novel. Of course no fishing lodge or guide service wants to put too fine a point on this, but we all know that getting weathered in—sometimes for days at a time—is always a possibility.

In a lifetime of fishing I've been stranded in a lot of places—airports, hotels, fishing camps, friends' homes and (by far the worst) tents—and I've learned that the only way to avoid madness in these situations is to have a good book to read. I do now make it a practice to carry more than one book because getting weathered in is never in the plan and you can't know when it'll happen, how long it will last or how far you'll be from the nearest bookstore.

I once made the mistake of bringing just one book on a trip and, sure enough, that was the trip where I got stuck in Goose Bay, Labrador, for two and a half days because the float plane that was supposed to take me and A.K. Best into the camp was grounded by a steady, pounding rain.

Now if you don't drink and you can't fish, there isn't much for an outsider to do in Goose Bay except read, and I'd finished my book halfway through my first day of lounging around the hotel lobby waiting for the weather to clear. It was a novel by Scott Spencer based not too loosely on the career of Bob Dylan. Spencer is one of my favorite writers, but his novels are real page-turners and I breezed through this one way too fast. It was like greedily chugging your whole canteen of water in the desert with days yet to go.

So there I was, a chronic reader stranded in an outpost in the rain without a book, and I had more than a week ahead of me. God knew how many days I'd be stuck in either a cheap hotel by the docks or a cabin out in the woods, and of course there was the long flight home that would take the better part of two more days.

So I set off alone, on foot, in the rain, to try to locate a book. Preferably a good one, although by then any book printed in English would do. It was a long, wet, lonely hike during which several locals stopped and kindly asked me if I was as lost as I looked.

I finally located a single, revolving wire rack of paperbacks in a drugstore. I passed up the bodice-ripping romance novels that are apparently popular up there and chose a Louis L'Amour knockoff Western and a foreign intrigue potboiler that didn't look all that interesting but was two inches thick and would last for days. They both turned out to be poorly written and way too predictable, but they were better than nothing.

On the hike back to the hotel with my precious books tucked safely under my rain slicker to keep them dry, I ran into some friendly locals who had an elaborate, homemade potato gun. I managed to kill the rest of the afternoon swatting mosquitoes and launching spuds into the Churchill River.

The rain never really stopped and the float planes

stayed grounded, but we eventually took a chartered heli-copter into the camp, where we got out almost every day and caught plenty of brook trout and char. I read myself to sleep every night with the potboiler (it worked better as a sedative than as literature) and inadvertently learned how to write a popular novel: You alternate scenes of vio-lence and sexual tension, more or less evenly spaced and constantly escalating, with just enough plot and charac-ter development to keep it from being entirely gratuitous, all fast-paced and visual, like television. It looked so easy that I briefly fantasized a new career.

When we flew out a week later, I left both books in camp, unfinished, because I was sure I remembered a bookstore at the airport in Montreal, where we'd have a two- or three-hour layover. And I never again made the mistake of going on a trip with just one good book that I was already halfway through.

Over the years I have reduced picking road books to something like an art form. You might think you should read a fishing book on a fishing trip, but that usu-ally doesn't work for me. If things are going well and I'm getting out on the water every day, I'm probably getting enough fishing. If not, a fishing book just underscores what I want to be doing but can't.

It's also possible to overload yourself with book learning. I may read up on a place or a kind of fish before a trip, but when I finally go, I like to leave the instructions at home so I can see and learn for myself and pick up ideas from guides and other fishermen, both of whom of-ten catch fish in ways the book said wouldn't work. There are some truly fine how-to-fish books in print, but even the very best of them are several notches below actual fishing.

I do make an exception for fishing books that are about more than just fishing and that are so well written it almost doesn't matter what they're about: *Trout Madness* by Robert Traver, *Dark Waters* by Russell Chatham, *Silent Seasons*, an anthology edited by Chatham, *The Longest Silence* by Thomas McGuane, *The Habit of Rivers* by Ted Leeson, *My Secret Fishing Life* by Nick Lyons, *Brook Trout and the Writing Life* by Craig Nova, to name a few.

I also have a soft spot for books that have little or nothing to do with fishing, but that have the unmistakable stamp of writers who are experienced outdoorsmen: *The Congressman's Daughter* by Craig Nova, *Just Before Dark* by Jim Harrison, *An Outside Chance* by Thomas McGuane, *Seasonal* by Ed Engle, *The Meadow* by James Galvin, *Justice* and *Montana 1948* by Larry Watson, and *The Summer Guest* by Justin Cronin.

Compared to those and others like them, most instructional fishing books aren't what you'd call beautifully written, nor do they have to be. I mean, when you read the directions for your new DVD player, you're not looking for insights and imagery, you just want to know which buttons to push to make the thing work.

Everyone's taste in books is different, but I think the best book to read when weather keeps you from fishing is one that's engrossing in some other direction entirely, like a complicated psychological novel set in a large city where, as a friend recently said, "nature is the thing you have to deal with between the lobby and the cab." That way, when you glance out the window or through the tent flap to see trees leaning in the wind, horizontal rain, and canoes filling with water, you'll be more likely to think, What the hell, a free day to do nothing but read isn't all bad. When you glance up from a fishing book, you're more likely to curse your fate, which we all know is a waste of time.

But whatever you decide to read, do it wholeheartedly. After all, if you're curled up somewhere with a good book in the middle of a fishing trip, the decision has been made. If you could be out there braving the weather and catching fish, you'd already be out there.

I bring either novels or collections of short stories or essays, but usually nothing by an unfamiliar author. Even close friends whose judgment I trust have recommended some real dogs, and there are few things worse than being stuck with a bad book when you can't either put it down and pick up a better one or go fishing.

Some of my favorite road books are the atmospheric crime novels by James Lee Burke featuring his signature character Dave Robicheaux, a philosophical, alcoholic, ex–police officer who runs a bait shop in Louisiana and owns a three-legged raccoon named Tripod. In the course of describing a scene, Burke might mention that you could smell the bluegills spawning, and when a case gets too complicated, Robicheaux will sometimes motor out on the bayou to catch bass and think things over. That's a nice touch, especially since he doesn't tell you *how* to catch bass.

Remember that when you read a book in a state of enforced isolation, it can begin to get into your head in ways that it might not at home. This can be good, bad, indifferent, or just interesting.

I was once stuck in Montana with one of those wisecracking tough-guy novels by James Crumley. One night at a café the waitress brought our check and said, "Now don't forget the tip, boys, 'cause I got a lotta mouths to feed." Without thinking, I said, "Honey, I'm already supportin' three waitresses back home": exactly the kind of smartass remark Crumley's detective would have made. It was far from the dumbest thing I've ever said, but it was weirdly out of character. I guess it's just as well I hadn't been reading Hunter Thompson.

I'll also sometimes go fishing with a book I read once and liked and have been thinking about reading again. Rereading a favorite book is one of the great literary pleasures, and doing it far from home in strange surroundings is sort of comforting, with its recalled passages and the familiar voice of the author. (At home my books are organized in a way that wouldn't make sense to anyone else and sometimes even eludes me, but it has something to do with books I won't reread, those I might and those I can't wait to read again.) I'll almost always discover new things in a book the second or third time through it, although sometimes the biggest discovery is how imperfectly I remembered it from the first or even the second reading.

Apparently it's not unusual for a book to be liked but poorly recalled in some way. Once I was sitting in the Salt Lake City airport waiting for a flight to Kalispell, Montana, when a guy with a rod case came over and said he liked my books. "My favorite one of yours is *Live Water*," he said. He's right, it's a great fishing book with a wonderfully evocative title, but I didn't write it; Tom McGuane did. I thanked him anyway.

I rarely pack more than one book by the same author unless I'm on a real jag. If things go wrong and you end up doing a lot of reading when you should be fishing, two back-to-back books by the same writer can begin to wear thin. Writers inevitably repeat themselves, and you may begin to see that a favorite author's lifelong theme is something as simple as "I don't understand women." You think, Yeah, me neither, and the spell is at least temporarily broken.

As a practical matter, it's best to carry paperback books on fishing trips because they're small and light. I love hardback books for their luxurious, permanent feel, and I've been known to take them on long driving trips where I have plenty of room, but when weight is a consideration, I leave them at home and bring the smallest, cheapest paperback editions I can find. Remember that if your weight limit on the float plane is fifty pounds, two hardback books can equal an extra change of clothes and a spare reel.

Paperbacks are also expendable enough that when you finish one you can just put it down and walk away from it without a second thought. Ed taught me that. He's a writer, fisherman and avid reader who buys cheap, dog-eared paperbacks at used-book stores for traveling, and when he finishes one, he just leaves it wherever he happens to be at the time: an airplane, hotel lobby, café, airport, fishing camp. He says it's one less thing to carry back home, and since hell is waiting forever with nothing to read, he figures he might be saving the sanity of some other poor stranded traveler.

Like almost all the readers I know, I started early

and with help. When I was little, my mother read to me from books like *The Swiss Family Robinson* by Johann David Wyss. This was before the days of "age-appropriate" books, when parents and kids just decided for themselves what to read, and I remember the book being a little over my head at the time, but I liked it anyway. Even if I didn't fully understand some of those early books, they made me want to be someplace else, gave me a sense of narrative and a lifelong curiosity about what was gonna happen next.

It was Dad who gave me books like *Grizzlies in Their Backyard* by Beth Day, *The Ranch on the Cariboo* by Alan Fry, and *African Hunter* and *Hunter's Tracks*, both by John Hunter (get the pun?), as well as books by Jack London, Zane Gray and others I've forgotten. I don't know exactly what he had in mind, but Dad taught me to fish, hunt, read a compass, build a fire and various other antique, manly skills I still use. He also gave me books that promoted a kind of irresponsible wanderlust at the same time he was trying to train me to be responsible. He couldn't have planned it, but in the end I was not successfully indoctrinated and eventually grew up to be a fishing writer. I can't be sure, but I may even have taken up fly fishing in my twenties simply because of its literary overtones. I think it was Arnold Gingrich in *The Fishing in Print* who said there have been more books written about fly fishing than about any other sport.

Those early books made me a lifelong reader, but they also set me up for being a mediocre student because what I came to think of as *real books* were so much more fun than the dull tomes we were force-fed by teachers. I don't know about now, but back then public education seemed designed to make children hate books as things that led through hours of drudgery to mind-numbing tests followed by lectures about failure. As punishment, a teacher might require extra reading. What kind of message was *that* supposed to send?

I did my own reading anyway, eventually with the help of Mr. Smith, a friendly, subversive young high school English teacher who once asked me, "Don't you ever wonder what's in those books the school board doesn't want you to read?" I did wonder, now that he mentioned it, and I vividly remember getting in trouble in a high school study hall for reading *The Way of Zen* by Alan Watts because it hadn't been "assigned." There were also difficulties with Robert Ruark's *The Honey Badger* (too racy), Woody Guthrie's *Bound for Glory* (too radical) and *Howl* by Allen Ginsberg ("Isn't he that Jewish homosexual?").

I also read *On the Road* by Jack Kerouac, in which the author predicted that soon millions of young people would be wandering America with packs on their backs, searching for the truth. That was in my senior year in high school, and the following summer I was wandering America with a pack on my back thinking, Imagine that— a guy says it in a book and it comes true.

I guess my reading has always been haphazard but passionate, sort of like my fishing. I decided early on that it's perfectly okay to like a book that a certain kind of reader would call "unimportant" or to honestly not get an acknowledged classic (the kind of book Mark Twain once defined as "often praised, but seldom read"). Neither means you're stupid.

I also learned that it's possible to come and go on books or authors over time. When I was in my teens, Ernest Hemingway literally changed my life, along with the lives of half the boys in America, by saying what we needed, or at least wanted, to hear at the time, especially in the Michigan stories, where the hairy-chested world-weariness was nicely combined with lots of fishing and canoeing. But then as I grew up, he began to fade for me a little. I think a lot of the later criticism of Hemingway was unreasonable (how could this lout not be sensitive to what we'd become sensitive to fifty years later?), but some of it was closer to the truth. Jim Harrison said Hemingway's apparent lack of emotion made him "a woodstove that didn't give off much heat," and maybe some of his later books *did* read like parodies of the early ones. A reviewer once said that *Across the River and into the Trees* should have been called *Across the Street and into the Bar.* On the other hand, *The Old Man and the Sea*—his last novel—is the best fishing story ever written.

I read that again a few years ago after visiting Hemingway's old house in Key West—now a museum—and buying a new edition of it at the gift shop there. My friend Pat and I were in Florida on a bonefishing trip and had arrived at that inevitable day when we couldn't go fishing because of the weather. We'd innocently gone down to the dock that morning in a howling gale, and our guide said we weren't going out in the little sixteen-foot flats boat. "There are small-craft warnings posted," he said. Then he pointed to a yacht the size of a house, adding, "And *that's* what they mean by 'small craft.'"

And so it goes.

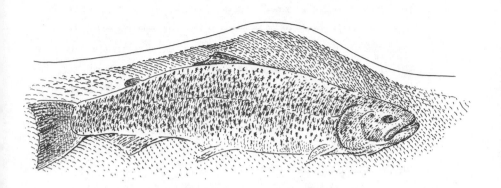

8. The Best Trout Stream in the World

Driving across Montana on the interstates, you can now intermittently pick up public radio stations from the Idaho border all the way east to Billings, then south through Sheridan, Wyoming, and right on down to my back door in Larimer County in northern Colorado. I always try to get public radio on the road, not because it's an absolute guarantee of quality (you can listen for twelve hours straight and still not hear a single song by either Greg Brown or Bob Dylan), but because it saves me from the two other likely alternatives: country and western, and rock and roll.

I could happily listen to country and western back in the days when it *was* country, but now that it's just rock and roll with cowboy hats, it rubs me the wrong way. Rock and roll itself—the genuine article as heard on the ubiquitous "classic rock" stations—gets it for me in a big way, but, as with many other good things, I have to be careful with the dosage. After even just an hour of high-volume head banging on a solitary, multiday, heavily caffeinated drive, I can catch myself going ninety-eight miles an hour while trying to chew my own teeth.

Of course up until fairly recently, I could have gone ninety-eight with impunity because Montana was the only state in the Union that didn't have a posted speed limit. "Reasonable and prudent" was the only daytime rule, although I do remember once riding in a pickup that was stopped by a cop who asked, as if he were just passing the time of day, "Don't you guys think a hundred and three is a little excessive when you're towing a drift boat?" We explained that we were going fishing. He asked where and we told him. He wished us luck and told us to "Just take it easy."

But Montana finally tumbled for the standard seventy-five-mile-an-hour speed limit under the threat of losing its federal highway funds. This probably made the roads a little safer, but it was also another step toward the kind of forced cultural homogenization where people with a distinct regional character are portrayed as nothing more than a bunch of dangerous misfits. Even when I was just passing through, I used to enjoy being in one of the last places in America that hadn't been entirely domesticated. Oddly enough, the arrival of law and order on the state's highways roughly corresponded with the proliferation of public radio stations, but I'm sure that was just a coincidence.

Anyway, I was up on a pass somewhere, temporarily out of radio reception and going a reasonable and prudent eighty-some miles an hour, when I caught myself wondering if I'd just fished the best trout stream in the world. I quickly shook off the thought because it wasn't really mine; it was just an involuntary echo of the media-driven obsession we have with the biggest and best, with everything else somehow falling short, even though "everything else" constitutes the day-to-day arena where we finally either locate happiness or not.

Where I'd been was in a small boat on a medium-sized river where the trout were uniformly the biggest I'd ever seen. I can't tell you the river's name or where it is because the man who invited me to fish it with him asked me not to. I agreed sight unseen (the invitation might have been rescinded if I hadn't) and it was the kind of promise that's sacred among fishermen. I guess I can safely say it's somewhere in the North American West within about a hundred miles of the U.S.-Canada border, never mind which side.

This was an obscure stretch of river where boat access is so problematic that it's hardly ever floated. Hiking in and wade fishing isn't out of the question, but it's a difficult enough proposition that not many people do it, and this is big enough water that even the best fly caster ends up leaving most of the water untouched when fishing on foot. But my friend, whom I'll call Ralph, had worked out a sneaky but still legal way to get a boat in there, opening up a lot of otherwise unreachable fishing. When we'd first talked about it, Ralph told me the trout were unusually big here because it's big, rich water that doesn't see many fishermen. It was just as simple, and rare, as that. He also said that if I wanted to fish it, I should do it soon because it had become sort of an open secret locally and people were bound to start sniffing it out before long.

Most don't come right out and say that, but when the subject turns to great fisheries that have so far been overlooked, the idea that time could be running out is often lurking just out of sight. I think that explains the expression of tight-lipped determination you see on the faces of so many fly fishermen these days. If you're even marginally in the life, you can hear about a dozen places every year that you really should fish before you die, or before they're discovered, whichever comes first.

We always seem to be looking for places that aren't used up yet so we can begin to use them up in our own small, modest way. Most of us are careful and none of us do any appreciable damage by ourselves, but hordes of us are a different story, and word inevitably leaks out because there are few fishermen so cagey that they can take their secrets to the grave. Add to that things like the threat of global warming and a U.S. population that just topped three hundred million with no end in sight and an element of quiet desperation can begin to creep into any way of life that depends on quiet, unspoiled country.

Ralph and I had met by chance while fishing for strange new fish in a strange place far from both our homes, and we hit it off the way fishermen sometimes do. There's no telling what he thought of me, but I took him as anything but your usual self-promoter. He was a professional guide, but I knew he wasn't giving me a sales pitch because no money would be changing hands and he pointedly did not want publicity for himself or the river. Still, I mentally reduced his claims of fish size by a third to avoid automatic disappointment. You know what I mean: we insist on making detailed plans for the future based on unreliable information, and then when a perfectly good but alternate future arrives, we say, "What?"

So I made the trip and in four days on the river, catching a respectable number of fish each day, I landed exactly one trout under twenty inches long. All the rest ranged from twenty-two to about twenty-six, with a matched pair—a rainbow and a brown—that were both twenty-eight inches. Ralph had said that once in a blue moon someone lands a thirty-incher there, but only a damned fool would quibble over those last two unlikely inches.

I'm not much of a fish measurer or even a very good guesser, but I'm confident about the size of these things because of Ralph. He's fished here for years and has seen other fishermen who'd also had trouble wrapping their minds around the scale of things. So on our second day on the river, when I had my fifth or sixth trout in the net—a rainbow that was comparatively on the small side—he staged what I suspect is a standard demonstration.

"How big do you think that one is?" he asked.

"I don't know," I said, "eighteen inches?"

Ralph already had a tape out and he quickly laid it against the trout. "A little over twenty-two," he announced.

Ralph said I wasn't the first to make that mistake, but it's still an odd phenomenon, since like most other fishermen, I tend to guess high instead of low on fish size. I think it's just that when they're all so big, your mind struggles to recalibrate on the spot and gets it wrong. I should point out that in virtually all of the places I fish, a wild trout that's anywhere near twenty inches long is a real showstopper and many of those twenty-inchers would actually tape out at seventeen or eighteen if anyone bothered to measure them.

These fish weren't pushovers and sometimes they were pretty difficult, but not in the bored, snotty way of tailwater trout that are so used to artificial flies that they'll sometimes refuse natural insects out of general paranoia. Here it was just the wild hair trigger that lets trout survive in a world populated with fish-eating critters like the golden eagles, white pelicans, ospreys, great blue herons and river otters we saw daily. At even the slightest hint of anything unusual, they'd either bolt for cover or just quietly vanish. There's no human comparison short of combat.

There was a good mix of water types—riffles, runs, pockets and glides—but we found a lot of our fish rising fastidiously in long, slow, glassy currents. It was usually a pod of three to five trout, all big, either bunched together or strung out, depending on the shape of the feeding lane. The rises would be quiet and delicate, but the bulges beneath them would suggest fish big enough to move a gallon of water with their backs. Ralph would ease the boat down with quiet oar strokes and anchor upstream, well off to the side and out of casting range. He'd lower the anchor slowly and wince if it banged along the bottom before we dragged to a stop.

The cast would be down and across current with an upstream mend and maybe another light tug as a final course correction. Then you'd feed a series of upstream slack mends into the drift, trying to keep the fly from dragging while at the same time not laying out too much loose line for a good set. I don't guess range much better than I do fish size, but a standard fly line is ninety feet long, and when I'd get a take at the end of some of my longest drifts, I'd be into the backing before I could say, "Oh shit!"

I wouldn't call this tedious fishing, but it was definitely time-consuming. At that range and current speed, a single cast and drift could take five minutes, and if your fly went by even a few inches to one side or the other of the feeding lane, it was doubtful that a fish would move to take it. Even when your drift was dead-on, the fish might ignore it because they were busy eating naturals, because they didn't like the fly pattern or for some other unknown reason. In any case you'd have to let the fly drift far past the rearmost riser so you could retrieve it for the next cast without spooking the whole pod.

It became obvious why all of Ralph's dry flies had prominent white or fluorescent orange parachute posts. That far out, the small size 16 and 18 dry flies we were using could dissolve visually even if you didn't blink or glance away for an instant, but you still had to know if a rise was to your imitation or a nearby natural. If you were wrong and a mistaken set ripped your fly across a quiet glide like a water skier, you'd blow up five beautiful, spooky trout, even the smallest of which could have the size and heft of an overripe zucchini. This is the kind of fishing that you can't rush, but at the same time you're aware that the trout will rise only as long as there are bugs on the water and that hatches don't last forever. You think you've remained calm until you realize you haven't taken a breath in almost a minute. Since we're going to release them anyway, there's no rational reason to be more excited about a big trout than a little one, but then a rational man wouldn't waste his life fishing.

With every hookup I was reminded that playing big fish is just like playing little fish, only more so. Setting the hook and coming up tight is still a definitive moment, but it's farther from the end of the drama than usual— more like just the beginning of act 3, where things could still go either way.

The trout liked my favorite little Pale Morning Dun emergers when they were feeding on that hatch, but I couldn't use them here because the fish were big enough to bend open the light wire hooks I tie them on. Even when I'd give them their head and manage not to do anything else wrong, the weight of a whole fly line and fifty yards of backing against the current was enough to do it. Ralph admired the simple fly anyway and said he'd like to try the pattern. I offered to tie him some when I got home—on heavier hooks more along the line of bent nails.

Morning hatches of pale morning duns, trikes and small, dark caddis were dependable, but these summer days would turn hot and bright and the bugs would usually peter out by one o'clock or so, but not always entirely. The river flowed through the kind of deep canyon where sparse hatches might continue to come off on the shady side of the river, and in currents that collected a lot of slow water into a narrower slot, there might be enough spent flies to get a few big noses coming up. Someone like Ralph who knew the river inside out could arrange to stretch the good morning dry fly fishing several hours into the afternoon.

When we'd finally run out of risers for a stretch, we'd switch to a rod already strung up with an ungainly rig consisting of a size 8 foam and rubber grasshopper followed by two small bead-head nymph droppers. There was one rocky, complicated bankside slot that was always good for a take to a dropper, though not always a hooked and landed fish. The twenty-eight-inch rainbow came out of there on that rig, and the persistent thought of the little size 16 nymph hook in that big bony jaw threatened to unravel me before I got it to the net. Of course there's no point in saying that except to imply that I *didn't* unravel and to mention again, just sort of casually, one of the two twenty-eight-inch trout I caught—in case you forgot.

This was clearly storybook fishing: the kind I once thought would be life changing but am now just as happy is not. When it comes right down to it, those fishermen who claim to have been spoiled by big fish have made life extremely difficult for themselves, and you suspect that they were actually spoiled rotten before they ever picked up a fly rod.

It's easy to get this whole business of big trout wrong. We do love big fish because of their scarcity, the difficulty of finding and catching them and for obvious reasons of vanity. (Those trophy photos we show off are really just portraits of our own egos.) When you're a young, gonzo fly fisher—simultaneously cocky and insecure and with adrenal glands as big as plums—you naturally gravitate toward the cult of size without giving it any thought, simply assuming that what you want from your life on the water are lots and lots of big fish. But then those rare days when something like that actually happens can later settle in your memory as the kind of greed riot you wish you hadn't indulged in.

In fact, large, wild trout should be caught in moderation, and it's possible to get enough really big ones that you'll finally begin to pine for your own little home water where, in just a few more days, a handful of eight-inch browns and brookies will begin to reestablish your sense of perspective. If you begin to wonder what it all means, as we all do from time to time, your first thought has to be that meaning is a human concept that's totally unknown to fish.

On that long drive home I casually watched my speed and listened to the radio news that I blissfully hadn't heard for the last week. (I pay attention to the news in the same way you'll stare at a terrible accident by the side of the highway: knowing you could see something you'll wish you hadn't, but somehow unable to look away.) Apparently things were as balled up as they'd been almost a week ago, only in a slightly different way. Unbelievably, the fact that a disillusioned news junkie had just had four of the best days of trout fishing in his life had not impacted world affairs one little bit.

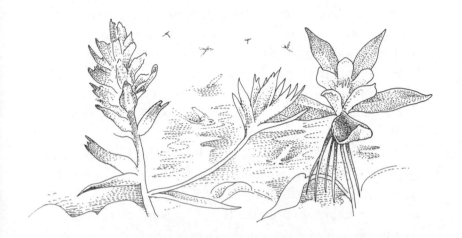

9. Flowers

Back in 1995, my friend Bob Scammell of Red Deer, Alberta, published a fascinating little book called *The Phenological Fly*. Phenology (not to be confused with "phrenology," which is the examination of bumps on the skull to determine character and intelligence) is the study of simultaneous natural phenomena like mating, nesting, leafing, blooming, whelping, migrations, insect infestations and such.

In a context unfamiliar to fly fishers, a mayfly, caddis or stonefly hatch could be considered an "infestation" instead of an occasion to catch fish, and what Bob did, simply enough, was to key the appearance of the major trout-stream insect hatches to the blooming of specific wildflowers along his local rivers. You could use other things that happen at more or less regular intervals, like the arrival or nesting of certain migrating birds, but flowers are good indicators because they depend on two of the same things that affect insect hatches, namely temperature and the length of the daylight.

This is one of those brilliantly simple ideas that have fallen out of favor now that we have hatch charts, Web sites and fishermen with e-mail and cell phones, but Bob reintroduced it as a way to fight what he calls "the malaise of modern fly fishing" in which everyone fishes in the same places at the same time.

The book's premise is that if you know a little botany and are even moderately observant, you can use phenology to predict the hatches and slip in early or, better yet, to find unknown hatches on uncrowded streams that other fishermen don't know about. You could also use the same sorts of correlations to predict the ripening of nuts and berries, the seasonal habits of game birds and mammals, when to plant certain crops and so on. This is the kind of knowledge that all people living firsthand in their own natural habitat once had out of necessity—what William Least Heat-Moon called a "deep map"—but that we've now mostly lost by spending too much time inside.

I thought of Bob and his book early last spring when I went to a nearby river to see if the blue-winged olive mayfly hatch had started yet. I went when I did because it was early April, when this hatch is known to begin at that altitude, but also because I'd noticed that the aspens and chokecherries around my house were beginning to bud.

That was one of two things I'd figured out on my

own in the decades before I read Bob's book and learned what phenology was. The other was that the bluegills would be spawning in some local warm-water ponds when the cottonwoods were beginning to leaf out and the Canada geese were on their nests. Both of those notions evolved over time as unquantifiable impressions that could pass as intuitions, but then after twenty years or more of being hit over the head with them, the particulars gradually emerged. I actually felt a little cheated when I learned that what I thought of as my own discovery was in fact an ancient science.

I drove up to the river on a day when you might not expect much of a hatch. It was bright and sunny and almost shirtsleeve warm at seven-thirty in the morning, while blue-winged olives are known to hatch best on cool, cloudy, drizzly afternoons, but the seasonal timing was right, so a few mayflies were coming off anyway. There were just enough duns on the water to get a few fish feeding—there were so few bugs, in fact, that I might not have noticed them except for the handful of rising trout—but I managed to catch several rainbows and a brown in a few hours on a size 20 parachute dry fly.

Oddly there were almost no other fishermen on the river, and this is one that can get crowded during the well-known hatches. That may have meant that my phenological observations had given me a head start on the hatch, or it may just have been that it was a midweek workday and not good enough olive weather to make anyone want to call in sick.

When the hatch petered out at around eleven o'clock, I thought about going home to do something productive, but being on a river with a rod in your hand generates too much inertia to resist, so I wandered downstream to check out some faster pocket water. There were no mayflies and no rising trout, but I fished the water with the same dry fly—casting to where I thought trout should be—and caught a few more from bankside slicks and the smooth tails of plunge pools. The usual explanation for this is that the insects have been hatching for a while, the trout are used to looking for them and they'll eat one if they see it and it's convenient. (As a fisherman, it's your *job* to make it convenient.)

I went to the river that day to scout the olives because the timing was about right for the hatch, but I hadn't heard anything about it yet and I think I would have. I'm not plugged into the information superhighway to the extent that others are, but if you've lived and fished in an area for more than half your life and have some equally technophobic friends, a telephone and the local café will still keep you on the grapevine.

When I finally got home late that afternoon, I called three friends to announce that the blue-winged olives were on. (The grapevine swings both ways.) It was news to all of them, although they weren't surprised. I also consulted *The Phenological Fly* out of curiosity and found that the spring blue-winged olive hatches in Bob's backyard in Alberta are also associated with opening aspen buds, even though that part of Canada is a thousand miles north of here. I even went to the trouble of keying out the Latin name (thank God for guidebooks) and found that it's exactly the same species of tree: *Populus tremuloides,* or what we call quaking aspen.

But then maybe that's not so surprising. Central Alberta is a long way from northern Colorado, but we're still at opposite ends of the same bioregion, in the same continental mountains and well within the range of both aspens and blue-winged olives. Distance notwithstanding, we're separated only by artificial political boundaries.

It's been said that on this continent, spring moves north at an average rate of seventy miles every four days, so you'd think Bob's olive hatches would come that much later than mine, but in fact the timing of both is roughly the same. That's because Bob's home waters lie in the neighborhood of 3,000 feet in elevation, while I live at 6,000 feet and the stream in question is at around 7,600. Since going up a mountain is the same as going north on the level, the difference in altitude effectively cancels out the difference in latitude, so the hatches come off at approximately the same time. A different kind of intelligence than mine could probably work this out mathematically, but I'd rather just go look at the aspen trees.

Of course any trout stream outside the Rocky Mountain West would be a whole other story, and Bob is careful in his book to point out that you can't use his keys unless you live in his part of the world because your local plants and bugs are likely to be different, not to mention the possible associations between them. Wherever you live, this is the kind of knowledge that once existed in specific detail and that was passed down regionally by word of mouth, but unless you can find a geezer who still remembers the old ways, you'll probably have to rediscover it for yourself.

It took me only a few minutes to compare *The*

Phenological Fly with the index in a guidebook to regional wildflowers and my own uncertain knowledge of hatches to learn that we have some of the same combinations here: western March browns and clematis, salmon flies and dogwoods, golden stoneflies and wild rose, green drakes and marsh marigolds. That is, we have the bugs and we have the flowers, but I didn't know if they had the same associations or were even found on the same river drainages.

I've always been more of a bird guy than a flower guy anyway, and the only blooms I knew were the most common and obvious ones. Columbine is the state flower. Monkshood (in the wolfbane family) looks like a monk's hood. Indian paintbrush sort of resembles a brush dipped in red paint. With some imagination, elephanthead looks like bunches of tiny purple elephant heads on a stalk, and so on. But it became clear that if I wanted to dabble at this, I'd have to learn a little more about wildflowers.

The beginning was the Indian paintbrush and columbines I noticed later in the year when I saw the first flavilinea mayflies on the water. The flavs are a long and productive hatch here. To a fly tier's eye they're a green drake, only a size or two smaller—or maybe a blue-winged olive, only a few sizes larger. The duns sputter off in the afternoons for weeks at a time, sometimes building into huge red quill spinner falls in the evening, and they work their way upstream in small, rough creeks that drop at an average rate of a hundred fifty feet per mile. The bugs move upstream slowly, so they're on somewhere for the entire high-country season.

The wildflowers also bloom progressively uphill, possibly at about the same rate, although I'd never paid much attention. On the other hand, the flowers I knew the names of were the ones I saw the most, and I saw them the most because I was on the water during the hatches. It was another one of those cases where you actually know more than you think you do because of the effects of peripheral vision and constant exposure, even if you're not entirely aware of it. All I knew *consciously* was that in years past, on especially good days of dry fly fishing, I would sometimes come to a spot where I could see 13,000-foot snowcapped peaks at the head of the valley through a gap in the woods and the banks were carpeted with familiar blue and red wildflowers. I'd stop fishing for a few minutes and think, Well, here I am again, catching trout in the most beautiful place on earth.

I *have* paid attention to edible wild mushrooms, though, or at least the precious few easy ones I'm sure enough of to eat. (I have nothing against flowers, but my Germanic practicality predisposes me to give prettiness a back seat to good free food.) The small pinecone morels come out in June when the streams are in full runoff, but I know that at some point when the flavs are on in August there can also be a flush of boletus mushrooms and, rarely, a little golden patch of chanterelles. The chanterelles are the most valuable (right up there with morels) and you can sell a bag of them to a fancy restaurant for a small fortune. The firm, nut-flavored boletus are more blue-collar and not as coveted by connoisseurs, but they go better with brook trout. It should be said that it's difficult to tell one wild mushroom from another, and many are poisonous, so you should never eat one unless you're absolutely sure of your identification.

I'm thinking of two or three small, pink-fleshed brookies lightly salted and peppered and fried in garlic butter with some sautéed boletus on the side, cooked in the same pan. You gut the trout and hang them in the cool shade for half an hour so they stiffen slightly and don't curl up from the heat of the pan—just long enough to get a spruce twig fire down to coals. The thickly sliced boletus should go in the pan within a minute or two of the trout being done so they stay almost crunchy. The mushrooms you want are the smallest, firmest, freshest ones. The species can grow as big as a dinner plate, but if they're much larger than a doorknob, they'll be soft and wormy.

So anyway, I spent the rest of that season making some observations that were just a little less casual than the ones I make anyway in the normal course of paying attention to my natural surroundings. I started carrying a wildflower guide in my daypack, although I used it more when I was off by myself than with company. After all, a fisherman who's seen *ooh*ing and *ah*ing over wildflowers when the trout are rising could be thought to have gone a little soft.

I learned the names of some new flowers by re-identifying them a dozen times until the common names finally began to stick and some naturally made more sense than others. For instance, there's a flower here known to botanists as *Grindelia squarrosa* (I had to look that up), but when you pick one of the small yellow blooms and it sticks to your fingers, you'll understand why it's commonly called gumweed.

But there are lots of flowers, so my private nomenclature crept back in with others. There are the tall, spindly red ones and the little white ones with yellow centers that grow in bunches near the ground. That kind of thing. It's the same way I privately think of the hatches: the little gray mayflies and the big tan caddis, never mind the genus and species. It *is* satisfying to know what things are called, but if you fixate on names to the exclusion of context, you can be guilty of what the artist M. C. Escher once described as "being interested in the gate, but not in the garden that lies beyond."

I sort of knew what to expect with flowers because I'd gone through the same thing at least twice before with fly fishing and bird watching. When I decided to learn how to fly-fish, it didn't occur to me that I'd still be learning more than half a lifetime later and still sometimes screwing the pooch as definitively as I did on my first day. When I took up noncompetitive bird watching, I thought I already knew most of the birds—you know, robin, crow, sparrow, blackbird, blue jay, barn owl and a few others—but it turns out there are well over six hundred species of bird in North America. Who'd have thought?

In other hands, the wildflower business could have turned into a full-blown, multiyear project with overlaying hatch, bloom, season and altitude charts and color photos like the lovely ones in Bob's book showing the actual insects perched on the actual flowers in question: impressive examples of both photography and bug wrangling.

In my hands it quickly became like bird watching, which is the kind of thing most of us do as a way of becoming more familiar with the particulars of a place, but with no other profit motive in mind. It's just that the

soul of a region is in the details and there are those of us
who believe it's pointless to ask "Why am I here?" until we
know where we are, which can turn out to be a life's work.
When some of us see birds, we simply want to know what
they are and what they're doing, but I can't think of a single instance where a bird has helped me catch a trout,
although I can think of times when birds have messed
me up. Once a raven threw his threatening shadow over a
skittish brown trout rising in shallow, clear water and the
trout (which I'm now certain I could have caught) bolted
for cover. I knew it was a raven before I looked up because
of the size of the shadow and the guttural croak. I also
knew that some ornithologists think ravens are intelligent
enough to have a rudimentary sense of humor.

For that matter, I now know the hard way that if
you cook yourself that rare treat of brook trout and mushrooms and leave it to cool for a minute while you go look
at the creek, you can come back to find gray jays—also
known as "camp robbers"—eating your lunch.

I didn't go too far with mushrooms once I learned
the common handful that are edible and that I like, as well
as a couple of poisonous ones like the fatally psychedelic
amanitas. Now and then, I'll find these with little chew
marks on them from pine squirrels. That seems odd, but
it could explain the hyperactivity and the constant chat-
tering.

I also tumbled to something else I'd known all
along without being entirely aware of it, which is that
the good fishing in the local high-altitude creeks roughly
coincides with the presence of hummingbirds, which in
turn corresponds to the presence of flowers. We have four

species of hummingbird here: rufous, calliopes, a few black chins and the ubiquitous broadtails. The hummers start peeling out of the mountains in late August or early September because of the shorter days and colder nights and because the wildflower nectar they feed on is becoming scarce. When that happens, it means the fishing will begin to taper off within a week or two. In the summer I wear a bright red hatband to attract hummers for the few seconds it takes each one to figure out I'm not a big flower, so I immediately notice when they're not there anymore.

This stuff sinks in slowly with lots of time spent outside, but it does sink in, and I've always liked the idea that everything is connected in more than just a metaphysical sense. Most of the threads are too long and tenuous to comprehend, but it's obvious that everything dovetails seamlessly with everything else to the extent that individuals are expendable, while the valuable nutrients are recycled forever, which amounts to our one little shot at immortality. Beyond that, maybe it really is true that a butterfly can flap its wings in Indonesia and two weeks later there's a tornado outside Wichita. Someone should probably look into that.

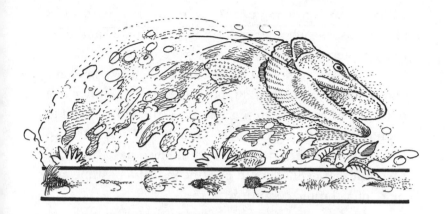

10. Musky

When Chris Schrantz and I went to northern Wisconsin in late spring to fly-fish some rivers for smallmouth bass, we were told that there could be muskies in the mix, but we honestly didn't think we'd see one. After all, Chris and I both grew up in the north country—just across the border in Minnesota—so we knew the mythology: Muskies can grow to enormous size, but they are all but impossible to catch. They were called "the fish of a thousand casts" and that was putting it mildly, since there were true stories of musky fishermen having fishless weeks, months and even whole seasons. The prevailing notion was that a big musky could be the fish of a lifetime provided you didn't go insane before you caught it.

Of course neither of us had fished for muskies while we were growing up. We were just kids with short attention spans who needed to catch a fish now and then to stay interested, while muskies were reserved for gray-haired guys with thousand-yard stares, Zen-like patience and no visible means of support. It was yet another one of those serious adult things that we were told we'd get to soon enough, so don't be in too much of a hurry. If we'd been paying closer attention, it could also have been our first hint that fishing could become less of a pastime and more of a chronic condition.

I don't know if my dad ever fished for muskies or not. I don't remember hearing about it and of course didn't bother to ask while he was alive and I still had the chance. I think he might have, though, based on a single piece of evidence. Among all the bass and pike lures in his old tackle box, which I still have, there's a single fourteen-inch-long jointed musky plug: an antique wooden one that I'm told would be worth a bundle to a collector if it weren't for the chipped paint and teeth marks.

So anyway, when one of the people we'd be fishing with, Mike Janeczko, said we might catch a musky by accident while fishing for smallmouths, I assumed it would be about as likely as spotting an ivory-billed woodpecker: just barely within the range of possibility, but not something you could plan on.

But then something else Chris and I didn't count on was how pervasive the musky vibe would be. We were staying in a borrowed apartment over the fly shop in Hayward, Wisconsin: a town that could qualify as the musky capital of the world. The National Fresh Water Fishing

Hall of Fame is in Hayward, and its centerpiece—for better or worse—is a perfectly proportioned, four-and-a-half-
story-tall fiberglass musky that looms over the small town
like something out of a 1950s horror movie. You can enter
the thing through a door near the anal vent, climb a steep
staircase through its gut and stand in an observation deck
in its open jaws.

More to the point, many record-book muskies
were caught nearby, including Louie Spray's sixty-nine-
pound eleven-ounce behemoth that has stood as the all-
tackle record since 1949. (A later seventy-pounder caught
in 1954 was disallowed because of certain "discrepancies"
in the weighing procedure.) There's at least one reproduction of Spray's musky at a local resort, and the skin mount
of the actual fish is hung in a place of honor down at the
Moccasin Bar.

In fact, we never went into a tavern or café in the
area that didn't have multiple large muskies hanging on
the walls. (There were also a few twenty-inch-plus smallmouth bass that were damned impressive in their own
right, but which, given their surroundings, couldn't help
looking a little like bait.) The regional aesthetic seems to
be that it's pointless to mount a musky weighing much less
than forty pounds, if only because it would be dwarfed by
the competition.

The majority of these big fish came from nearby
lakes or from reservoirs known as "flowages," but even
while you're fly-fishing rivers for smallmouth bass, the
musky business is always in the air. For one thing, you
can adequately fish for smallies with something like a six-
or eight-pound tippet, but because there are muskies in

the rivers and they're known to eat the same flies, you have to attach your bass bugs to your leader with some sort of bite guard or shock tippet.

I tried the forty-pound test hard mono that I've used successfully in the past for northern pike, but my first unexpected strike from a musky sliced it cleanly and I lost my bass bug. It was early in the trip and, if nothing else, I didn't want to spend the rest of the week feeding swimming deer-hair frogs to muskies at the rate of six dollars apiece.

The people we were fishing with (Mike, Wendy Williamson, Larry Mann and Mike Sergeant—a.k.a. Sarge) all preferred bite guards of sixty-five-pound PowerPro, a woven material that stands up well even to a sharp pair of scissors. I borrowed some and it worked a little better. That is, I lost the next two muskies that hit, but at least I got my fly back. Still, in the course of a week we lost several more flies to muskies that, as Chris said, bit the PowerPro in half cleaner than any of the tools we were using to cut it.

Most of the plug fishermen use wire leaders for muskies and it works well—although some say it cuts down on strikes—but I'd once tried wire leaders while fly fishing for pike and came to the same conclusion as a local fisherman, who said, "I'd rather just lose flies than try to cast wire on a fly rod." Clearly further research is called for.

Another difficulty with muskies is the strength of their jaws. They can grab a fly and hold it so tightly that, however hard or often you pump the rod, the fly won't slide in the fish's mouth, which of course is how you set a hook. (Plug casters say a big musky is strong enough to crush a treble hook.) Muskies are tenacious predators and they'll sometimes hold on to your fly through a good run, during which you can assume they're hooked. But when they finally decide that this thing they've attacked is more trouble than it's worth, they'll simply open their mouths and let go of the fly. Your bite guard held, you'd hit the fish "hard and often" as you'd been told by the guides and you'd even played the thing briefly, so you couldn't help but feel cheated.

The only other rule was, never stop retrieving your fly, no matter what happens. They say a musky immediately loses interest when the prey stops fleeing, while on the other hand, there are stories of them following a lure so far that they run into the boat with an audible thunk.

I should say that the smallmouth fishing was excellent. The fish catching was steady, if not nonstop, and they were wild, pretty fish of all sizes, including a few pushing twenty inches, almost all caught on top-water bugs. It was what we came for and what we spent most of our time doing, but after several strikes from muskies without even trying, things began to take the inevitable left turn. Before it was all over, we'd spent two days floating a river that's known as good musky water.

I won't mention the river's name because we were kindly taken there by friends and it's not my place to publish its location, especially since musky fishermen are about as secretive as you'd expect. Big muskies are known to take up residence in a specific area and spend much of their lives there. When a truly dedicated fisherman discovers one—whether it's by getting a follow, missing a strike or spotting the thing lurking in the shallows—he can make a career out of trying to catch it, while going to equally great lengths to keep its location to himself. While we were there, a guy got a big musky from a local flowage, a trophy in the fifty-pound class. He posted a photo of it on a Web site, but he had obviously superimposed the image of him holding his fish over a postcard view of the Canadian Rockies in order to disguise the location. We heard about this from several people who all thought that was perfectly understandable.

The nuts and bolts of fly fishing for muskies turned out to be fairly straightforward. Muskies are said to like riffles—and I did get one vicious pull in fast water—but these are placid rivers that don't *have* many riffles. We actually moved most of our fish in fairly quiet, knee- to thigh-deep bankside water, usually with a jumbled, rocky bottom, a nearby drop-off and some kind of good cover like large rocks, sunken logs or brush piles. They came to the same flies you'd use for smallmouth bass—patterns resembling minnows, crawdads and frogs—and those critters were exactly what we saw while wading that kind of water during pee stops and coffee breaks.

I'd always assumed that musky lures had to be as big as that old clunker in my dad's tackle box because most of them are. On our first night in town, Chris and I walked over to a local bait shop to buy our nonresident fishing licenses and to look at displays of musky plugs costing upward of twenty-five dollars each, bristling with treble hooks and bigger than most of the trout we catch back home in Colorado. I know these things work be-cause they've been in use for generations, but the smaller flies that worked for us made a kind of day-to-day sense, too. After all, there's no reason to think that your average musky is any different than your average wolf. The great wolf biologist Farley Mowat said that wolves might prefer to bring down full-grown deer, but in order to stay fed their diet consists mostly of mice.

According to the late Al McClane, the fish's proper name, muskellunge, comes from the Ojibway words *mas* and *kinononge,* meaning "ugly fish," and that's how most of the big ones are mounted: with their heads thrown back in a hideous snarl showing off thousands of snaggly teeth. This is done to celebrate the heroism of the fisherman who caught the thing. (They say you could lose fingers or an entire hand; some trophy musky fishermen carry side-arms.) Taxidermists put muskies in the attack pose for the same reason you'll never see a grizzly bear mounted in the act of contemplatively picking lint from his navel.

I have a photo of Chris holding a forty-five-inch musky—a smallish musky, but still a big fish—and wearing that mildly dazed expression you sometimes see in snapshots of fishermen. He's slightly amazed that he caught the thing and, in a larger sense, equally amazed that they can be caught at all on a fly rod. But then I never trust people who try to act as if catching a nice big fish is no big deal for a sportsman of their stature. After all, fishing is nothing more than the often successful search for something genuine in a world where we're increasingly comfortable with things like coffee "creamer" that's guaranteed to contain no actual dairy products. We're so used to the fake and the packaged that encountering something real can amount to a borderline religious experience.

That day, Chris and I landed three muskies between us and missed or lost at least that many more. (So they're not the fish of a thousand casts after all. I'd say no more than six hundred casts per strike, tops.) We naturally handled the fish carefully, as you would anything that's large, strong, slippery and has lots of sharp teeth. In the course of a week on several different rivers, we got strikes from maybe two dozen muskies, most of them on those two ten- to twelve-hour days when we were actually fishing for them. Some bit us off and many of the others simply came loose. Still, we landed just enough to prove that, although fly fishing for muskies isn't exactly mainstream even in this part of the world, it's not that unusual either. The locals were always excited when one of us would land one, but they weren't the least bit surprised. This literally happens every day.

At this late date it should come as no surprise that some fishermen somewhere are successfully doing whatever you can think of, not to mention plenty of things you can't. (Once a guy called to say he'd perfected fly fishing for prairie dogs. As soon as I determined that he wasn't joking, I told him not to call me again.) So when I got home and someone said, "Really, muskies on a fly rod?" I said, "Well, yeah, why not?"

Naturally it wasn't lost on us that there were much bigger fish in the river than the ones we were catching: that gnawing truth that eventually dawns on all fishermen and musky anglers in particular. If the mounts back in Hayward weren't enough, we saw one jump in a midstream riffle that was better than twice the size of anything we'd hooked, and I landed a yard-long musky with half-healed bite marks on him from a set of jaws that were seven inches wide, suggesting a mouth that wouldn't look out of place on a fair-sized alligator. Larry said that was probably from the recent spawn, which can get a little rough. Like all fishermen, I have some sympathy for the fish, and getting nearly bitten in half by a larger rival makes my own troubles with love look pretty tame.

During the course of landing, admiring and releasing the first musky I actually got to the boat, I got excited and somehow lost the long-handled hook disgorger my dad had given me some forty-five years ago while we were pike fishing. This was the oldest piece of fishing tackle I had that I still used, and at the time it couldn't have cost more than twenty cents. It probably went over the side, since it wasn't in the boat when the commotion died down and that was the only other possibility. I had a brief Dad's-gonna-kill-me moment before remembering that he's long past caring, and even if he weren't, he'd be proud of me for holding on to the thing for so long, only to finally lose it in action.

This is how time occasionally works. One minute you're a thirteen-year-old drowning worms for bluegills because muskies are among the countless things that are out of your league; the next minute you're a decently preserved fifty-eight and finally landing a musky. Surely all kinds of things have happened in between, but at the moment you can't remember any of them.

11. Cheap Dates

I was on a river in western Colorado with my old friend
A.K. doing what you could call a job. A.K. had written a
new book about fly fishing and it had fallen to me to take
a long series of color slides showing him demonstrating
all kinds of specialized and sometimes complicated casts.
You know the kind of photos I mean: the ones where not
only do the light, focus, shutter speed, background and
composition all have to be anywhere from adequate to
flawless, but the fly line must be frozen in the air at precisely the right point in the cast to illustrate the text.

It was a game of exquisite timing. The difference
between tripping the shutter too soon, too late or right
on time was infinitesimal, and although A.K. really can

perform difficult casts over and over again, the constant repetition under pressure would occasionally cause him to blow one. The manuscript called for sixty step-by-step captioned photos. I won't tell you how many rolls of film I burned to get them.

That was the week it rained steadily on the East Slope of the Rockies, while over on the West Slope we had clear, calm, bluebird mornings that were perfect for photography, followed by cloudy, blustery afternoons with scattered rain squalls as gobs of that eastern monsoon front peeled off and oozed down from the Continental Divide. By two o'clock on most days, the unsettled weather became useless for the kind of photos we were after, but not half bad for fishing.

So that's how we came to be on the river at a time of year that isn't particularly popular with fishermen. According to the published hatch charts, the spring midges and blue-winged olives were over by then and the green drakes, red quills, pale morning duns and tricos were yet to come. So what we had on those stormy afternoons in late June was a deservedly popular river with almost no other fishermen on it. At first glance, it seemed both inviting and eerie. You think, Oh boy, there's no one here. Then you think, *Why* is there no one here?

But trout-stream food chains grind along at their own uneven but steady pace. The fish still have to eat, and, as usual, the dead spot on the hatch chart is never quite as dead as you're led to believe. During that week the last of the small blue-winged olives—the size 22s—were still petering off in scattered pockets here and there and the first of the pale morning duns were just starting to emerge a week or two ahead of schedule. Both hatches were sporadic and on the thin side—with one all but over and the other just barely beginning—but they were there, and if you hit it right, they'd overlap, with enough bugs on the water to get isolated pods of trout moving to the surface.

There were also the incidental bugs that randomly sputter off any trout stream in summer but which no fisherman would call a "hatch": some caddis flies of various sizes and the usual odd smattering of midges, mayflies, crane flies, ants and beetles.

We even saw the occasional early green drake, even though the main head of this famous hatch was said to still be weeks away and far downstream, all the way out of the river we were fishing and miles down the *next* river. I'd have said there weren't enough of the big drakes around to interest the fish, but then A.K. was casting a size 10 White Wulff dry fly for the photos (the wrong color for a drake, but almost the right size) and most mornings he'd get a few odd strikes on it. After a few days of that, he sheepishly clipped off the point of the hook so catching trout wouldn't distract us from our photography chores.

We developed a routine. After a morning of shooting photos, we'd drive the thirty miles to the nearest town in A.K.'s pickup and drop off the film at a lab that, for an extra fee, would process the slides in a little over an hour. After a long lunch we'd go over them using the lab's loupe and light table, deciding what was done, what was left to do and what we wanted to reshoot. More than once—against all odds—I managed to get flawless shots of every cast A.K. flubbed and none of the good ones.

(And yes, I know there are those who would have

used a digital camera and a laptop and that it would have been a lot more efficient that way. But A.K. and I both prefer the look of film, and when you're faced with a big job, you automatically reach for the familiar old tool. In this case that meant the venerable old Pentax K1000s we've both used for decades.)

Anyway, after we'd gone through the day's slides, we'd drive back up to the river as the sky clouded over and the afternoon rain squalls began to build. The calm air and the good morning light would be gone, the mid-day summer doldrums would be over and the dull shadowless light and cooler temperatures would have some bugs emerging and a few trout moving. The running joke became "Well, hell. I guess there's nothing else to do but go fishing."

This was a roadside river that made for easy scouting, so most days we'd just drive along at a fraction of the speed limit, scanning the water and stopping at every turnout until we found a few rising trout. Sometimes it was a nice long run or a series of plunge pools where there was room for both of us to fish. Other times it would be a single slick that we'd take turns on. Your turn would be up when you caught a fish, missed a strike or had to change flies. (The rules changed with the conditions.) Now and then we wouldn't be able to find any risers, so we'd just go to a good-looking run and wait for a hatch. Either way, the river was all but vacant, so we had our choice of spots.

A.K. is a fairly serious dry fly fisherman, so he often *would* wait: watching the water, going pensively silent and puffing on one of those stinky little black cigars he likes, sometimes with the hood of his rain jacket up to keep off the spitting rain. Once he stood silent and motionless in a single spot for a full half hour, asleep on his feet for all I could tell. Then he calmly waded in, made a single cast with a size 16 Pale Morning Dun and noodled a sixteen-inch brown trout from under an overhanging limb against the far bank. This was the only trout that rose in fifty yards of river in the space of thirty minutes. Talk about precision.

I usually lack that kind of patience, so after a while I'd get antsy and wander off either to pick up a trout or two on a brace of nymphs (usually a size 16 PMD with a size 22 Olive on a dropper) or maybe work slowly downstream swinging a nondescript, medium-sized wet fly through the runs and pockets.

Swinging wets on a tight line is an ancient method that still works, as sloppy and unscientific as it seems by modern standards, and that delights me. Some fishermen who have rediscovered it in recent years can spout theories about why it works—it imitates a swimming caddis pupa, for instance—but I think it's a simple matter of trout psychology. That is, your average trout is like your typical barn cat: tightly wound, perpetually hungry and operating on the predatory rule that if it runs, you should chase it and kill it and then see if it's good to eat. In other words, you swing wet flies for the same reason that you should never run from a bear or a mountain lion.

Done properly, wet fly fishing takes lots of room. Like an Atlantic salmon fisherman or a steelheader, you make your cast, fish out the swing, take two or three steps downstream and repeat the process, making lazy roll casts and covering the water methodically. You shuffle along at a casual pace, but after an hour of fishing when you decide to go back and see how your partner is doing, you're amazed at how far you've gone. These days fishermen are more likely to stand in one place and pound the water with nymphs until their feet go numb, not so much because it works well, but because on too many crowded rivers there's no room to do anything else.

The same would be true here later in the year, but the midsummer fishing was supposed to be poor, so just about everyone was elsewhere chasing the main event. It was fun trying to sniff out the odd bank riser that might eat an ant or beetle, or the occasional short, sputtering hatch, or to provocatively swing a wet fly through a few hundred yards of river, not copying anything in particular or expecting to clean up, but just prospecting for the odd trout with a short fuse. It was also luxurious to have all the room we could ask for to do that.

More and more now, A.K. and I enjoy this kind of moderately slow fishing where a trout or two can certainly be caught, but where you can't count on much more than that. After all, the one place you almost always want to be is on a trout stream with a fly rod in your hand. Once you're actually there, it seems unreasonable to impose further conditions.

The more common view of the sport now is that it is, or should be, one big fish-catching spectacle after another, while those odd and delightful opportunities in between are too often referred to as "poor fishing." But there's a specific beauty to a well-known trout stream between those big hatches that will attract more fishermen than fish. It's not showing off for company now, but just padding around in slippers with a cup of lukewarm coffee, waiting for something interesting to happen.

Of course A.K. and I will happily rise to the occasion if things unexpectedly start to get exciting, but it's easy enough to fall back into just being two old friends fishing together, both of whom, through sheer force of time spent, have long since caught their share of trout. That doesn't mean we're done by a long shot, only that the pressure is off.

So we eventually shot our sixty photos and got in some fishing, too, which was sort of how we'd hoped it would go. We also lived high on the hog in a rented cabin because A.K. had managed to charm his publisher out of an expense account to cover room, food, gas, film and processing. It was a pretty posh cabin, too, with a full kitchen, a satellite TV that we didn't watch (couldn't figure out how to work it) and two bedrooms separated by a short hall and two heavy doors: enough space and lumber to muffle A.K.'s hideous snoring so I could get some sleep.

I have to say I enjoyed the whole setup, although having my tab covered as the official project photographer made me feel competent one minute and, if not fraudulent, then at least out of my depth the next. (There are better photographers than me for this kind of thing, but none of them would work for room and board.) I *have* published some photos over the years—mostly spreads with articles and a precious few old magazine covers— and I always thought unposed shots taken by competent amateurs gave those publications an authentic, journalistic feel. But in recent decades as fishing magazines have gotten slicker and real professional photographers have entered the field, those of us who could once sell a reasonably informed snapshot have begun to fall by the wayside.

And why not? After all, a good photo is a long way from a great one and, as too many art directors have told me, my "models" (my friends, that is) are too old and dopey-looking and are fishing with tackle that's years out of date. I mentioned that once when we were all around a campfire together and got precisely the response you'd expect.

These days I usually leave the cumbersome old Pentax at home and carry a small, light, waterproof Canon Sure Shot that I use for the occasional big-fish photo. Days of fishing can now go by before I shoot even a single frame, and I don't mind that one bit. If nothing else, there's a photographic equivalent to the Heisenberg effect whereby taking the picture changes the event and I've started to think there's value in leaving some things undocumented.

So this is how I once imagined life as a fishing writer. I knew that even success would only make me a big fish in a little pond—which isn't all bad, by the way. I also knew I wouldn't get rich (fly fishing is a good way to *spend* money, not make it). But I did think maybe I'd stay in log cabins with all the amenities, whiling away my days with a little work and then some fishing, while some vague publisher somewhere paid the bills. It almost never actually works out that way, and even when it does, there's always an annoying catch. Still, some people do make assumptions about professions they're unfamiliar with.

Once I was down at the local feed store, and one of the guys on duty that day said, "Settle a bet for us. You actually get paid to go fishing, right?"

"No," I said. "I mostly fish on my own dime and then get paid to write about it."

The guy thought it over for a minute and said, "Oh yeah, I guess that *is* different."

People having slightly skewed ideas about what you do for a living isn't a burden or anything, and in fact it can lead to some interesting insights.

I went to a shoe repair place a few years ago to have some hiking boots resoled, and when I gave the man my name for the work order, he said, "You're the guy who writes that fishin' column in the newspaper, aren't you?"

I modestly admitted that yes, it was me, and he turned to the man next to him behind the counter and said, "Well, the guy wore out a pair of boots, so it can't *all* be bullshit."

To prove some obscure point, A.K. had wanted to come in under the estimated budget on the expense account, but as time went on, it looked like we'd come in too far under, so we'd planned to make up the difference by going into town at least one evening while we were there to eat an expensive dinner. There was a restaurant we'd heard glowing reports about for years, but we'd never eaten there because we couldn't afford it.

This would have had something to do with being honest and diligent and getting the job done, but still coming away with a little harmless swag before it was all over. Never mind that when you have a job that requires you to do lots of fly fishing, most people think you've already successfully beaten the system—and they're probably right. They may also assume that your so-called professional status makes you either more or less of a real fisherman, or maybe just puts you off to the side in some vague way. I'm probably too close to this to comment intelligently, although a fishing writer I know did once describe the refreshingly innocent attitude of a friend of his by saying "He's not in the business: he's a nonprofit fisherman."

As it turned out, though, the fancy dinner never happened. There was the pricey restaurant just a few miles down the valley and there was the wiggle room in the expense account, but in June the sun sets late on the West Slope and the evening fishing can be the best of the day, so dinner would always end up being a thermos of coffee and ham sandwiches on the river. A.K. and I have been at this a long time, but try as we might, I guess we're still cheap dates.

12. Hunt

I had to come back early from the combined deer and elk hunt this fall for reasons that were crucial at the time but which aren't important enough to go into now. The upshot was that one morning I got up at five o'clock along with my hunting partners, Ed Engle and DeWitt Daggett, and we went through our habitual ceremonies: before breakfast, Ed does twenty minutes of tai chi, DeWitt does yoga, I drink coffee and smoke cigarettes. But then when they walked out the door of the cabin carrying rifles in the predawn dark, I restocked the firewood, did the breakfast dishes (a laborious affair involving buckets of river water heated on the stove), then packed my gear and left.

It was a sad moment, since those of us who really

do live to hunt and fish feel something has gone terribly wrong when that other life intrudes, however occasionally or unavoidably. So partly just to cheer myself up, I stopped halfway down the canyon to see my old friend Roy Palm, who had just gotten home from a bird-hunting expedition to North Dakota. He had pheasants and sharp-tailed grouse in the freezer and one of his yellow Labs had a bandage on her right front leg from a cut. Roy gave me the usual rib-cracking bear hug and the dogs wiggled and fawned the way they do, but they settled down quickly because they were still tired from hunting.

Roy naturally asked how it had gone, and I said that, as of that morning, no one had killed anything. We'd seen a few animals at long distances or in fleeting glimpses, and I'd passed up a shot at a deer that I wasn't sure I could make. It was a long offhand snapshot, and as I mounted the rifle and thumbed off the safety, the Voice said, "Well, you can hit it, but you can't be sure *where*. You could be out here for days tracking a wounded animal and eating your guts out." (This takes longer to repeat than it did to hear. The Voice speaks in a kind of shorthand.)

I was disappointed without being regretful. What passes for my religion now is informal and atavistic, but in situations like that I can still fall back on the stern old Midwestern Protestant ethic I was brought up on. That is, if not doing something involved a conscious act of self-control and really cost you what you wanted, then you probably did the right thing.

The three of us have been hunting this unit on the edge of a wilderness area in western Colorado for the last fifteen years. Its biggest advantage is that DeWitt has the use of a small cabin there. It's a comfortable place with an adequate kitchen, a fireplace that could be a little more efficient on cold nights and a porch that acts as a drumhead, amplifying the footsteps of anyone approaching the front door.

The hunter who's been out all day without firing a shot plods, while the guy who has an animal down prances the last few steps as he prepares to deliver the news and the long story that goes with it. In DeWitt's case the animal is invariably clear the hell and gone up the mountain, and when he gets around to describing where it is, the size of the dawn-to-dusk chore we'll be faced with in the morning begins to take shape.

Sometimes there will have been foreshadowing in the form of a shot heard during the day from a direction where one of us said he'd be hunting. We're usually not the only hunters on the mountain, but—at the risk of bragging—a single, definitive report is more likely to be one of us than is the panic-stricken four- and five-shot volleys you sometimes hear.

The cabin is in an "undersubscribed" big-game unit, which means there aren't as many hunters as there are in some places, so you can usually draw whatever licenses you put in for. We typically go for doe deer and cow elk tags, plus maybe an additional bull elk license bought over the counter, just in case. We all hunt primarily for the food and espouse the meat hunters' credo of "You can't eat the horns," although I've heard it just as convincingly the other way around: "You'll still have the antlers to admire long after you've forgotten how tough the meat was."

But then the unit is undersubscribed because there aren't as many deer and elk as there are in some other areas and also because the country is steep and rough as a cob: definitely not ATV-friendly (thank God), occasionally problematic for horses, and even a little difficult to cover on foot in some places.

It's an ideal area for somewhat younger hunters (like we all were when we started hunting here), but by now we know it so intimately that every difficulty amounts to a hidden advantage and we can't imagine hunting anywhere else. It's also been good to us. The hunting can be laborious, game is sometimes hard to find, and getting the meat out can be a grueling chore even with DeWitt's packhorses, but there's only been this one season in the last fifteen when no one got anything. Since we split the meat evenly, there's always deer, elk, or some of both in everyone's freezer. That adds the pleasant pressure of hunting for others as well as for yourself. It's pleasant because you could get to feel the pride of the provider, but if you fail, no one actually starves.

I've effectively hunted all my life and now, as I approach sixty at what seems like breakneck speed, I'm either better than I've ever been or at least as good as I'll ever get. In other words, I feel that I'm an adequate hunter, with my best skill being that I understand my limitations as a marksman and hunt well within them. I've never shot anything at more than a hundred yards, but then I've also never had to shoot anything more than once. On the other hand, I tend to hunt in thick woods where you can rarely *see* a hundred yards, so it all works out nicely. A few of my kills have been the result of pure

craft and stealth, while a few others came simply by virtue of being outside in season with a loaded rifle. Most
fall somewhere in between.

Age can slow you down a bit—not always a bad
thing for a big-game hunter—and it can also reduce your
effective range. I've noticed that in recent years I've spent
most of my hunting time in a familiar stretch of moderately rugged country that's pretty close to the cabin and
covers only a few square miles, but which apparently
holds inexhaustible possibilities. A taste for the habitual
becomes comforting after a while, but it can also be useful. For instance, it took me a long time to work out how
the elk travel along this slope, but I eventually zeroed in
on it and have now killed three within a half mile of each
other, all at roughly the same elevation.

As long as he stays active year-round, an experienced hunter is more likely to be aware of his physical
shape and to know what he has in the way of reserves.
In my experience an older hunter is less likely to get into
trouble and more likely to get out, provided that getting
out doesn't require extreme acts of strength or endurance.

At a certain age you're also a little less prone to the
kind of excitement that can border on panic when things
get serious and can open a black hole into which all kinds
of things fall, including good judgment. That's why, for instance, the first thing you do when you're sure an animal
is down is to unload the rifle.

The hazards of this kind of hunting are no less
real for being perfectly ordinary: loaded firearms, razor-
sharp knives held in cold hands and the homely possi-

bility of tripping and breaking a leg. On the other hand, success and failure are often separated by things like the shuffle of hooves in dry aspen leaves, the flick of a deer's tail at seventy-five yards or maybe going up this draw instead of that one for reasons that you may or may not have learned in the last decade and a half. Eventually you begin to pay equal and profound attention to everything, large and small, before, during and after the actual hunt. In time, that can settle into the kind of stillness that could conceivably follow you home from the woods.

I'm primarily a deer guy, and I hunt elk as if they were just big mule deer. That's true only in the taxonomic sense, but I've still managed to get a few. My first elk brought on the usual storm of emotions. At first it was "Oh boy, I got one." Then, as I walked up on the six-hundred-pound carcass, it was "Holy shit, what have I gotten myself into?" And then there was that inevitable moment of regret over killing a fellow animal who was only trying to make a living. (Russell Chatham once wrote that a fisherman can always release a fish, but in hunting "success is irreversible.") I won't make too much of this, but everything that's good to eat was once alive, including vegetables, and all primary cultures have observed that tragic aspect of food gathering in one way or another. Which is to say, if I ever lose my respect and sympathy for the game I hunt, I hope someone takes away my rifle and sends me to bed without supper.

For at least the last dozen years now, deer and elk hunting has easily been the hardest work I do in a year's time: not so much the hunt itself as the considerable chore that begins when you kill something. I actually enjoy that part because it's all about the true nature of killing and hard work as the origins of food—life and death as pure biology. The main problems with buying meat wrapped in plastic in a supermarket are that you don't have to leave at dawn with knives, bone saws, ropes, and packhorses, and when you get home, you're not cold, tired, sore, and bloody.

The sense of being part of a continuing process caused me to develop a little ritual. I like to go back to the site of a kill to see what's been feeding on the gut pile. The gray jays and mountain chickadees arrived while I was still field-dressing the animal, but if there's tracking snow down, I can later find evidence of assorted mice and wood rats, weasels, ravens, coyotes, bobcats, and maybe a pine marten. Once, after only a day and a half, the whole pile of guts from a cow elk was gone: probably the work of a black bear. The gut piles left by hunters in the fall have become a part of the ecosystem, giving all manner of scavengers the gift of a well-fed head start on the long winter. Nothing is ever wasted.

DeWitt also started a small ritual of his own. He didn't feel right about tossing the leftovers from skinning a deer (the hide and hooves) into a dumpster, so he started returning them to the woods where they'll be nutrients instead of just more human garbage. Ed and I immediately adopted this informal rite because it seemed properly respectful, never mind that the sight of a grown man throwing deer legs into the trees at sunset looks like something out of a French art film.

I do hunt a little less avidly than I once did, now limiting myself to deer, elk, blue grouse near home, and maybe a hike or two up into the thin air at eleven or twelve thousand feet for ptarmigan: unassuming little birds that are as succulent as quail but twice as big. That wasn't exactly a conscious decision, but things do sort themselves out as life progresses. Some of the best steel-head fishing of the year happens during the fall hunting seasons, not to mention the best dry fly fishing for trout, and it became obvious that I was a fisherman who also does some hunting rather than a hunter who also fishes.

But I do still hunt, and when someone occasionally asks me why, it occurs to me that the only reason we have brains large enough to formulate that question is that our distant ancestors got the extra protein it took to evolve the organ by supplementing their diets with meat, first as scavengers, then as hunters. Hunting made us who and what we are. It's in our nature more deeply than clothing, tools, or language. Other than that, I can't think of a good reason.

So that's what it takes to put in a winter's meat, and of course the meat itself is better in every way than anything you can buy. It's lean, flavorful, low in cholesterol and has no additives (a dream come true for every organic food Nazi, including those who don't approve of hunting). Doing your own killing, the work that follows and a humble ritual or two also strike me as morally and maybe even spiritually superior to the modern alternative. A visit to a feedlot or slaughterhouse will quickly turn any sane human being into either a hunter or a vegetarian.

Of course the horses make the job easier than it

was when we packed meat out on our backs—and for me they complete a childhood fantasy about hunting in the West—but horses also add an element of incipient chaos. Until we started using them on the hunt, my direct experience with horses was limited to being posed for a photo on the back of a docile Shetland pony when I was five or six years old, but even DeWitt—who is an experienced horseman and farrier by trade—admits that these animals sometimes puzzle him.

For instance, why would Cookie step confidently over six inches of exposed culvert on an old logging road, while the inappropriately named Sweetie spooks and throws a tantrum that finally puts her on her back with all four legs in the air? Possibly because Sweetie is a Missouri fox trotter and thinks being a beast of burden is beneath her dignity. A horse can be honestly frightened by something as benign as a culvert, but it's also capable of only *pretending* to be afraid.

But then Cookie had some tense moments in the beginning, too. The first time DeWitt brought her on the hunt, she was a young saddle horse formerly owned by a little old lady who only rode her to church on Sundays. She was skeptical about the sight and smell of her first dead elk, not to mention her growing suspicion that we planned to put half of it in the panniers on her back. Even if you don't know a lot about horses, those big round eyes amount to a kind of universal body language.

But DeWitt said that as long as we loaded the more experienced Honey first so Cookie could see it was okay, everything would be fine, and it was. In the end, she dutifully carried the lighter front quarters back down the mountain, where she got brushed, fed, and watered and acted supremely unconcerned about the whole experience. I gave her an affectionate rub and told her she was a good girl, but I'm not sure it registered. Cats purr and dogs helpfully wag their tails, but horses are harder to read.

13. Winter

About the time autumn ended last year and another three seasons had slipped away too soon, a friend announced, only half seriously, I thought, that he was getting too old for winter fly fishing: standing all day in water just above freezing, tying the smallest imaginable flies to tiny tippets with numb fingers and fogged magnifier glasses, often catching few if any trout . . . I thought, Yeah, me too, but I keep doing it anyway, and not necessarily because I'm so crazed that I *must* fish all the time, no matter what.

It's tempting to invoke George Mallory, who famously climbed Mount Everest because it was there, but winter fly fishing takes nothing more than stubbornness instead of actual endurance and courage. And of course Mallory couldn't just walk back to the pickup, run the heater and pour a cup of hot coffee from the thermos.

As often as I've tried, I've never been able to figure the odds in winter fishing. You know, what are the actual chances that you'll go fishing, hit everything more or less right—stream flow, cloud cover, temperature, hatches, and the ineffable moods of the fishes—and find some trout you're able to catch? Not that I've figured the odds for spring, summer, and fall fishing either, but there are fewer places to go in the winter and your chances seem notice-ably thinner, although it does sometimes pan out, and by sheer force of numbers it pans out more often the more often you go.

Based on thirty-some years of local winter fly fish-ing in Colorado and the same three decades of hearsay, I'd guess that if you went out every second or third day all winter you'd hit a dozen days that were about as good as it gets and about half that many more that were excellent. All the rest would be dogs in terms of fish caught, but still somehow a necessary part of the process. There are those who deal with that by fishing "ferociously," as they say, but I've noticed that the happiest fishermen I know have simply developed a definition of success that includes any trip they live through.

I naturally did more winter fly fishing when I was younger. I may have been a little more impervious to discomfort then, but more than that I was new to the Colorado Rockies and still delighted that it was not only legal to fish with rod and reel year-round, but that there were also a few stretches of open water—tailwaters and the odd spring creek—where you could actually do it with some hope of success.

Growing up in my formative years in Minnesota, I'd gotten used to a too-short summer fishing season and a too-long ice fishing season. I did ice-fish, but only, again, because it was there to do and because staying home to play Scrabble with your sister was for cream puffs. But even then it was painful and tedious. If you were sitting in the open on an overturned bucket gazing down a hole in the ice, there was the all-too-real danger of frostbite. If you were shut up in a dark shanty with a smelly kerosene heater, a bottle of schnapps for the men and hot chocolate for you, it was possible to die of boredom listening to the droning of the grown-ups while being told to be quiet yourself so you didn't scare the fish. The only advantage I could see was that there were no mosquitoes.

Fish were caught now and then—northerns, walleyes or maybe perch—and they were especially firm-fleshed and delicious when they came from cold water, but catching fish didn't seem to be the main point unless you were some kind of fanatic. In those days and in that place, the ice fishing shanty served the dual purpose of group therapy and the neighborhood tavern except that it was more socially acceptable than both. A real man would never seek help for an "emotional problem," but he might air things out with his fishing buddies, and although drinking in a bar could have some ominous connotations, drinking in an ice house was considered medicinal. There were times when I could tell by the tone of a voice or a sidelong glance that the men would have talked more freely without a kid around, so I'd act like I wasn't listening and try to learn something useful.

Growing up, moving to the Rocky Mountains and learning to fly-fish opened up a new window on winter fishing. After the inevitable slapstick of learning how to do it, fly casting was a lot prettier than staring down a hole in the ice, and wading and casting both involved movement, which is crucial in all winter activity. Waving a stick isn't enough exercise to keep you warm, but at least growing numbness and impaired coordination will tell you when you're cold enough to do something about it.

The best day of winter fishing I ever had was years ago in the Cheesman Canyon stretch of the South Platte River during a blinding February snowstorm. The day was so cold that every time A.K. or I would catch a fish, we'd have to go back to our bankside fire to melt the ice from our guides, thaw out our reels and warm our hands. We had the usual pot of coffee going and the first sip of a fresh cup would melt the frost in your mustache. But even with all that time off the water, we each caught at least two dozen nice-sized trout on size 20 Blue-Winged Olive dry flies, and as near as we could tell, we had the entire three miles of canyon to ourselves. It was still snowing when we left, and the drive home that night—which usually takes about two and a half hours—took more like five and it was only a kind of pigheadedness that kept us from checking into a motel to wait out the storm. We agreed that it was a glorious day of fishing and that we'd never knowingly do it again.

Common wisdom says the best days of winter fishing are toward the end of periodic thaws with temperatures above freezing—maybe even up in the high forties or briefly into the low fifties at midday—with an approaching low-pressure front that darkens the sky and spits a little light snow or drizzle. (Some fishermen think trout can feel the pressure change in their lateral lines, but the fisheries biologists I've asked say they just like the cloud cover.) Bright days are sometimes okay, not to mention more comfortable, but too much sun is likely to make the trout shy and keep the hatches down. Clouds, cooling air, wind and snow are usually better.

The best two days I had last winter were when Vince and I drove over to the Fryingpan River on the West Slope. It was gray, chilly, snowing steadily and there was a little more wind than you'd want for either comfort or fly casting. We drove over to the river in the morning, checked into a motel, stopped at a fly shop, filled a thermos with hot coffee, dropped in on a friend for a few minutes and then hit the water, where we found rising trout in the first pool we tried. To someone who grew up fly fishing the West, trout rising in a moderate snowstorm is only a pleasant, familiar sight, but as a transplant I'll probably never get over the amazement of it.

This was one of those perfect winter fishing days: dark and cloudy, breezy, with moderate snow and not quite too cold to fish. The thermometer at our friend's house had read 42 degrees at noon, but the wind-chill and humidity effectively lowered that by ten degrees to near freezing.

Still, it wasn't bad. We dressed for it with long johns, fleece, wool sweaters, down jackets, fingerless gloves and insulated hats with earflaps. (When you're fishing in winter—not moving around that much while standing in cold water—you dress two or three times more warmly than you would if you were hiking in the same weather.) We were only moderately miserable, with the inevitable running noses, numb feet and stinging fingers, the fingers made even colder by periodically chipping ice from the guides on our rods and releasing fish. Decades ago, winter fly fishing was a fairly specialized affair practiced by only a handful of true believers, but it has now caught on to the extent that some tailwater rivers are nearly as crowded in the winter as they are in the summer. But even though it's no longer anything special, there's still the temptation to go on about how uncomfortable it can be.

The trout were lying toward the head of the long, riffly pool feeding on a hatch of dark midges. We started with dry flies because many of the fish were showing in the head and tail rise that usually means they're eating either the floating, winged flies or the emergers right in the surface film. During some hatches you eventually have to go underwater with a pupa or nymph pattern, either as a dropper off the dry fly or with a little lead on the leader to sink it deeper, but I always try the dry fly first just because it's such a pretty way to catch trout.

That afternoon I got my fish on a size 22 A.K.'s Midge Emerger—a sentimental favorite pattern that I often try first. Vince got his on one of the Suspender Midge patterns he'd bought at the fly shop in town. These are two very different flies, but they're about the same size and color and the fish were eager, so that day they worked interchangeably.

The hatch petered off by about three-thirty, so we

wandered downstream to look at some small slicks and runs to see if any fish were still rising down there on what was left of the bugs. It seemed pretty dead, but then Vince located two good-sized trout rising to leftover cripples in a smooth back eddy. He had to wade waist-deep in fast current to reach the spot, and even then it was a tricky cast and a difficult drift, made no easier by the insistent wind. He hooked the bigger of the two after a few tries, but the fish broke the 7X tippet on the set. Then, with a fresh fly on, he hooked and landed the other trout, which turned out to be an eighteen-inch brown. All in all, it was a pretty nice job of fly fishing.

That night, watching the Weather Channel in our motel room, we learned that it had snowed hard that day back on the East Slope and that the passes we'd driven over easily that morning were closed by the storm. According to the TV weather map, the Fryingpan Valley was sitting in a milder backwater of the storm, protected by mountain ranges on three sides that took the brunt of the blizzard. It was brutal at higher altitudes, but down on the river it was ten degrees warmer, only moderately crappy and pretty much perfect for fishing.

It had also snowed hard just a few miles to the south in Aspen. Earlier we'd talked to a guy from a roofing crew down there who said they had to shovel six inches of snow off a roof before they could shingle it. It was windy and cold as hell, he couldn't feel his hands all day and he didn't much care for being two stories up on a slippery roof, but a guy has to make a living. I told him we'd spent the day fishing, but I didn't complain about the conditions.

The next day the weather held about the same: snowing like hell in the high country; threatening worse than it ever produced down in the valley. We drove to a different part of the river and went to a stretch I've always liked where, sure enough, trout started rising to midges ten minutes after we arrived. It was almost the same deal as the day before, with the bigger trout holding near the riffly head of the run and a few smaller ones down in the slower tail. It was also the same hatch of size 22 dark midges, so we felt pretty confident.

Vince caught four or five trout on the Suspender Midge right off the bat, but I wasn't doing well on the A.K.'s Emerger, although I managed to get one small rainbow on a size 22 Miracle Nymph fished behind it as a dropper. After ten or fifteen minutes, Vince offered me one of his flies, making it less of a big deal by saying "You've given me enough flies over the years." That did it, and we both caught trout off and on until, once again, the hatch petered out in mid to late afternoon.

We drove upstream then and tried nymphing a few more spots, but it was pretty much over. I managed to hook two small trout on size 22 Brassies, but both of them threw the hook. Vince never got a strike.

Then we drove even farther upstream to kill time by halfheartedly scouting more water and saw four other fishermen, two still in the water, casting without much enthusiasm, two more just getting out. Those were the only other fishermen we saw in two days on a normally crowded river. It's not that anyone was scared off by the weather; they just couldn't get to the river with the passes closed.

By four o'clock the temperature had dropped to

well below freezing, the wind and snow had both backed off a little and the river had gone completely dead. The low clouds had just begun to break apart, and in a few spots you could see thin patches of dark blue sky that would have stars in them in less than an hour. It would clear off completely overnight, and without that lid of overcast to hold in the meager warmth, the temperature would drop into the low single digits. I was beginning to think in terms of a hot meal in a warm diner. When you're out in the cold all day, your body burns calories like a bonfire, so as soon as you start to warm up, you become suddenly and desperately hungry.

We stuck it out for another half hour anyway, even with all but the faintest hope of catching a trout gone. There's nothing prettier than a deserted trout stream in the snow and since neither of us do that much winter fishing anymore, this could turn out to be the one good trip for the year. That kind of knowledge makes you want to linger a little.

And there was that good smell: cold, clean, antiseptic, slightly metallic, but still somehow organic. When I was a kid, I had a terrible adenoid infection—possibly caught while ice fishing—that left me with a seriously impaired and weirdly selective sense of smell. Flowers are lost on me, so are perfume, soap, most Dumpsters and many spices. On the other hand, I can smell new-mown hay, smoke and coffee, and once in British Columbia, I unmistakably smelled a grizzly bear on the downwind side of an alder thicket. And I at least like to imagine that I can smell a trout stream in winter.

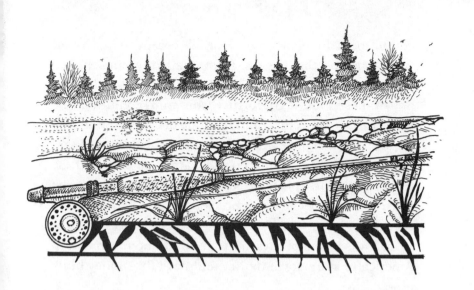

14. Rods

During one of those inane bookkeeping rituals where I had to make my life look more comprehensible on paper than it is in reality, I learned that my thirty-year accumulation of bamboo fly rods is now worth more than my IRA. I remember staring at the figures thinking, Surely this means something, but what?

There are those who'd say it simply means I've spent too much money and squirreled away too little, making the prospects for retirement look bleak, but I think it means that the whole bamboo rod business has finally gone over the top.

That would explain why I once put some of my favorite old bamboo rods out to pasture because they'd gotten too valuable to fish, then felt creepy about it and started fishing them again. I got conflicting, unsolicited advice on this. A collector told me that every time I fished one of these rods, it got further from mint condition (the holy grail for collectors) and its value decreased. But then an old friend rightly pointed out that a fishing rod you don't either use or sell has no value at all. I'd bought these things in the first place because I thought they were fine rods. If they'd become too precious to use with the passage of time, they were also too good not to—and fishing won. I was proud of myself. After all, it's no mean feat in America to stare down money and have the money blink first.

Rising prices could also explain why, although I've fished predominantly with bamboo fly rods for most of my adult life, the last four rods I bought were all graphites. If I felt I needed excuses, I'd have them. Two of those rods were fourteen-foot, two-handed spey rods, and that's a specialized configuration where graphite just outperforms bamboo. Honestly a bamboo spey rod—if you can even find one—might be stretching the point a little even for a purist. The other two were conventional nine-foot, five-piece pack rods (a 5/6 weight and an 8/9) that fit snugly into the duffel bag I check at the airport. At first I just thought of them as emergency spares, but on a recent trip to British Columbia I strung up the lighter rod for no other reason than that I'd brought it and ended up using it all week because it was just a really nice rod.

So one afternoon I was happily casting a foam stonefly pattern on a graphite rod when our guide said, "You know, if this gets out, you could lose your charter membership in the Old Farts' Club." Fair enough. I could rightfully say that I still do most of my fishing with bamboo and use graphite sparingly—for salmon and steelhead and on trips that involve psychotic baggage handlers—but those of us who fish bamboo inevitably generate reputations as curmudgeons and we're expected to take the heat graciously. All the more so when you presume to write a little book about bamboo rods as I once did. I met a man in eastern Canada recently who'd read that book and who said he was "shocked" to see me fishing graphite. I quickly went through a dozen possible responses and finally settled on something like "Well, what're ya gonna do?"

I'm not alone in straying. Several of my bamboo nut friends have also at least partially gone over to the dark side with graphite without apology. They say the bamboo rods they own now are incomparably sweet and irreplaceable, but that the prices of either new ones or good old ones are now both so prohibitive that they'll probably never buy another one. In fact, I know a man who once got into a financial bind and had to sell his old, and by then collectible, bamboo rods. When he got back on his feet a few years later and looked into replacing them, he found that he could no longer afford anything but graphite.

But then some graphite rods are magnificent casting tools, and in recent years that includes several that are very affordable even by modern standards. They aren't flashy and they don't carry lifetime guarantees, but they're cheap, they cast beautifully and they hold up to hard use, which is all you can ask for.

In the meantime, the cost of some new bamboo

rods by current makers equals or exceeds that of some collectibles, and the market in quality used bamboo rods has begun to simultaneously escalate and implode. The prices continue to rise, while the finite supply of rods by the famous dead makers steadily declines due to loss, hoarding and breakage, so the remaining rods recycle more grudgingly. A rod dealer once told me that he now depends largely on the widows of his former clients for his supply of classic rods.

The most desirable bamboo rods by the most renowned historic makers were fairly pricey when they were new and got pricier when they became collector's items. They've always been out of reach for all but a few, and apparently they're going to stay that way. Somewhere in middle age the realization arrives that you are making as much money as you'll ever make, so if you can't afford something now, it will always remain a carrot on a very long stick.

The so-called production bamboo rods that were once my forte have also gone off the deep end. Rods by the old Heddon, Granger and Phillipson companies always top this list, but there are at least a dozen others that are also perfectly good or even great rods that were affordable before collectors discovered them. Over the years I've come by a few big-name rods honestly, but I usually went with the bargains, and they *were* bargains. I can tell you from experience that, for instance, a model 208 Payne and a 9050 Wright & McGill Granger—both versatile 9-foot, 5/6-weights—are virtually identical except for the huge discrepancy in price.

But those good old production rods are now collectible, and their values are rising accordingly. The 8-foot, 5-weight Granger I bought used in 1976 has now appreciated by over 3,000 percent (a pretty good investment if I had the heart to sell it), and because of that its context has changed. If you drove a 1958 Ford in 1967, it meant you couldn't afford a newer one. If you drive the same thing today, it means you're wealthy enough to fool around with classic automobiles. The same goes for bamboo rods. Where a Heddon, Granger or even a vintage Leonard once made you a little old-fashioned, the same rod today makes you an elitist.

A friend who has fished bamboo rods for decades said that if he encountered them now—with their current baggage and price tags—they probably wouldn't interest him. I may or may not agree with that, but I do know what he means. By chance more than design, I managed to assemble all the classic bamboo fly rods I'll ever need back when I could afford them, and I doubt that I could live without them now. On the other hand, although I may be loyal, I'm not sure I actually mate for life.

If that were the whole story, bamboo fly rods would soon disappear except as curiosities. Eventually the few survivors would all be under lock and key somewhere, with any possibility of appreciating them simply as fly rods terminally crippled by their value. But there's been a quiet renaissance in bamboo rod making that has resulted in scads of new makers.

Most date that resurgence to the publication of *A Master's Guide to Building a Bamboo Fly Rod* by Everett Garrison and Hoagy B. Carmichael in 1977. That wasn't the first good book on the subject, but Garrison had become legendary by then and the book came at a time when bamboo had become a quaint backwater in the mass market, graphite was obviously here to stay and the mid-range classic bamboo rods that were still going for a song at flea markets were beginning to be noticed by collectors. It was the moment when bamboo was either going to quietly fade away or just as quietly come back. It came back.

I can't guess how many new bamboo rod makers there are now. In 1987, ten years after the book's publication, Hoagy Carmichael told me that, aside from the twenty or so "established" makers, he knew of at least a hundred others "working in their basements and garages." A few of those have since gone on to become established in their own right, and there are now enough obscure, part-time and hobbyist makers around that all you have to do is mention bamboo and a maker you never heard of pops out from behind the nearest bush.

I wouldn't know how to characterize these makers' attitudes, but they may be a little different from the nostalgic view I'm used to. A few years ago I interviewed a young rod maker who was just beginning to sell his rods at a local fly shop. I asked him the standard question, "Why bamboo?" expecting the standard answer involving tradition, craftsmanship and poetry. You know, if graphite is forced-air central heating, then bamboo is an oak fire in a stone fireplace.

Instead he said he was just interested in tapers and actions, didn't think there was anything special about bamboo and actually had a soft spot for fiberglass. But it takes a factory to make glass or graphite, while you can make a bamboo rod on the kitchen table with hand tools, which is exactly how he got started.

This guy's rods sold for what you could call an entry-level price for bamboo and they were surprisingly good, but he said he had no aspirations about turning pro. There was a family to support and he liked his day job. He just made rods for fun and sold a few to finance his own fishing.

From what I can tell, the part-time aspect is fairly typical of new rod makers, while the high quality early in the game may or may not be. In one sense, anyone who's patient, handy with tools, comfortable with extremely fine tolerances and doggedly meticulous can make a bamboo fly rod. In another sense, top-quality rod making is a rare and exceptional skill in which only a handful of crafts- men in a generation set the standard, and there are count- less fine points of design and execution that are learned only through long experience. A bamboo rod dealer who handles several new makers told me he figures the aver- age rod maker isn't worth much until he's worked out the kinks by producing at least fifty rods, and even that isn't a guarantee. On the other hand, there are savants whose second or third rod is as good as anything you'll find, re- gardless of age, price or pedigree.

The current bargain-basement bamboo rods are Chinese imports that have come on the market in the last few years. They're all said to be built on "classic" tapers and their prices are astonishingly low for bamboo: about the same as you'd pay for a brand-name American-made graphite. The few of these I've cast seemed like perfectly serviceable fly rods, although the finishes and fittings on

John Gierach

most of them left a lot to be desired and I can't say how they'll hold up to hard use. The one man I know who owns one says he fishes it often and likes it, but I haven't noticed a run on them.

That's probably because imported bamboo rods have never done very well in the United States. Up until now, most of those were English and they were made for European fly fishers, who have different ideas about casting than we do. There's also a kind of chauvinism in operation. We've always thought that the best bamboo rods were made right here, starting with Hiram Leonard in the late 1800s, and for political reasons, many just want their bamboo rods to be made in America, never mind that the bamboo itself comes from China, the silk from Japan and the fancy wood in the reel seat from a vanishing rain forest in Brazil.

Things are further complicated by a handful of rod makers who have bought or licensed the names of defunct golden age rod companies and are now reissuing bamboo rods that you could call reproductions, facsimiles, commemoratives or something like that.

I don't really have an opinion on these except that the one I've fished with was a nice rod, but I do see some potential problems for the makers. There will inevitably be comparisons to the original rods, and since the old classics are iconic, the standard will be impossibly high. Also, some of these new rods cost nearly as much as the originals, leaving a buyer to ask himself, Why get a reproduction when for a few dollars more I could have the real thing?

But then buying a well-known old name is one way

to get your rods noticed in a crowded market. From what I've seen, the happiest new rod makers are like the guy I mentioned earlier: part-timers with a local following and no ambition except to make the best rods possible. It's more of a struggle if you want to start making all or even part of your day-to-day living selling your rods.

I'm guessing at the figures, but I'd say that of that first generation of *Master's Guide* makers, a tenth stayed with it seriously for the next thirty years. Of those, an equally small fraction turned pro and are now success-fully competing with the surviving masters of the last generation, who somehow survived their own process of natural selection. As a craft, bamboo rod building is now a friendly and welcoming subculture, but as a business it has a high mortality rate.

Aside from trying to be noticed in a crowd, modern bamboo rod makers have other problems. For instance, several makers have told me there's a class of customer who cares more about cosmetics than about how the rod casts. This customer literally goes over a rod inch by inch with a magnifying glass and throws a hissy fit when he lo-cates a microscopic speck of dust in the varnish. When he calls to complain, it turns out he hasn't even cast the rod.

The client from hell usually claims to be a con-noisseur of the classics, but when I go over some of my own classic rods that closely, I can find plenty of so-called cosmetic flaws that wouldn't pass muster. So the bar for craftsmanship is probably set higher now than it's ever been, but that comes with the danger that rod makers will pay more attention to how their rods look than to how they cast.

Many bamboo rods are now sold to fishermen who have never cast one before, and I've talked to two rod makers who are trying to make their bamboo rods act and feel like graphite so they'll be more recognizable to those customers. I walked away from both conversations with the same unanswered question: If a fisherman likes graphite, why would he pay two thousand dollars or more for a rod that casts like one he could get for two hundred?

Thankfully, though, most modern bamboo makers still work from traditional tapers, as I think they should. (In the fine arts, you can break rules and still be considered successful, but in the crafts, a cup still has to hold coffee and a rod still has to cast.) It's an article of faith among the older generation that after well over a century of experimentation, there are no more than thirty basic tapers that work in bamboo. But then with so many of the great old rods now out of circulation, many new makers have never seen or cast the rods they're trying to reproduce. That's the main reason why you can try out half a dozen rods supposedly built on the legendary 7½-foot, 5-weight Payne number 197 taper and they'll all be different. (Another reason is that there are enough variations between culms of bamboo that it's virtually impossible for any one rod to be an exact copy of another.) Some makers do repairs and restorations on old rods, not only as a service to their customers and for a little extra income, but also as a way to get their hands on some of those classic tapers.

In practice, there seem to be three kinds of maker: those who stick faithfully with traditional tapers, those who don't and those who start in one place and end up in another by various routes. The common wisdom is that if a maker claims to have come up with his own new taper, the best you can hope for is that he's accidentally reinvented the Leonard Model 39-DF. But then there's the story of a rod maker who claims that his best new taper came to him in a dream—and who's to say it didn't? I've cast several of this guy's rods and they were all exceptionally good, so all I can say is, find out what he drinks and send a case of it to all the other rod makers.

I think bamboo rods are in a watershed now. There are more makers than there have ever been, the craft is alive and well and for those who have a weak spot for it, the aesthetic is firmly in place: A fine, handmade bamboo rod is not only pretty to look at and a joy to cast, but in the world as it is, it's also a victory of the handcrafted over the manufactured; the cottage industry over the corporate death star. The best bamboo rods may or may not equal the chilly efficiency of the best graphites, but even if they don't, their amiable gracefulness more than makes up for it. There's always some sentimentality involved in choosing an old technology over the new one, but it's almost impossible to isolate, so it's hardly worth mentioning. As for whether or not bamboo rods are worth the cost, that's finally up to the individual fisherman who decides to either buy one or not. There's a kind of casual rod shopper some bamboo types call the "whistling gopher." This is the guy who points at a rod, asks "What's that one go fer?" and then whistles loudly when he hears the price.

But modern builders turn out rods in much smaller numbers, and we'll probably never again see anything like the best of the old production makers who sold quality rods by the thousands per year. A man I know who has made bamboo rods full-time for the last quarter century just recently cracked six hundred rods and says he may not make a thousand before the end of his career.

Some modern bamboo rods are every bit as good as any ever made, but the landscape has changed, and without the household names and national reputations buyers once relied on, the good rods can be harder to distinguish from the rug beaters. It's probably true that most of the best rods are made by established professionals whose fame gets them the premium prices, but lower price doesn't necessarily reflect lower quality, and the affordable sleepers made by craftsmen known only to a few dozen local customers are well worth the trouble it takes to find them.

And, once found, good rods can still be hard to get. Some well-known rod makers are dependable, but have waiting lists that stretch out four years or more, and many part-timers produce rods on a limited and somewhat unpredictable schedule. The idea that you can want to buy something, have the money in your hot little fist and still not be able to get it is incomprehensible to many Americans, but instead of hurting the market, that only magnifies the romance. A man I met recently summed up the bamboo rod buyer's dilemma succinctly: "If you order a rod from a new maker," he said, "he might quit before he gets around to building your rod. If you order one from an old master, he might die."

15. Labrador

I was in the lobby of the aptly named Two Seasons Hotel in Labrador City, Labrador, when I heard about the latest terrorist scare from a fellow traveler. He said authorities had arrested some homegrown English extremists who were plotting to blow up commercial flights from the United Kingdom to the United States using liquid explosives smuggled aboard in tubes of toothpaste, bottles of hair gel and such. Security personnel had understandably gone into a state of hysteria and air travel had ground to a dead stop.

I'd just spent the last twenty-some hours flying from Denver to Toronto to Quebec to Sept Îles to Wabush without hearing a word about this, and it was somehow odd news to finally receive in a small coal-mining town effectively at the end of the road in northeastern Canada.

Anyway, I did what Americans do in that situation: I went back to my tiny room, found CNN on the television and settled in for an hour of the numbing repetition that now passes for news. Most of the details were still unknown, but the one undisputed fact was that airport security had clamped down hard and surprised passengers were being unceremoniously relieved of all liquids, gels, lotions, creams, ointments, aerosols and so on. (Exceptions included things like small doses of liquid medication provided the prescription label matched your I.D. and baby formula provided you could produce an actual baby.) Some passengers were just plain scared, while others felt ambushed by the sudden rule change. Either way, the resulting confusion was causing flight delays upward of seven or eight hours and live shots from airports looked like illustrations from Dante's *Inferno*.

I got the now-familiar ice-cold chill in the pit of my stomach because this could have been—maybe almost *was*—much worse. I even experienced a genuine moment of sympathy for those who were caught in this mess, but the sense of having dodged a bullet was overriding, so I mostly just felt lucky, which is the proper way to begin a fishing trip.

The next morning I boarded a forty-some-year-old de Havilland Otter float plane and flew a hundred kilometers or so north to Three Rivers Lodge on the Woods River. This was a homecoming for me because I'd fished at this place a few years before with Jim Babb and A.K. We not only caught many large brook trout, but also became friends with Robin Reeve, the owner, and Kevin and Frances Barry, the manager and head cook, respectively. There were hugs and handshakes all around, and at one point Frances took me aside and asked how Jim and A.K. were doing. Newfoundlanders have the habit of friendliness, but they're also a laconic bunch, so when she said "I thinks about you boys from time to time," I was touched by this outpouring of raw emotion.

The next day Robin, the sporting artist C.D. Clarke, our guide, Jimmy Whittle, and I flew another hundred and fifty kilometers north toward the Arctic Circle, where we planned to camp and fish on an Arctic char river for two days. The plane was an orange and white de Havilland Beaver. The pilot was a man named Marco, a brash French-Canadian who enjoys saying things like "Don't worry; if we run outta gas, it won't be by much."

The conditions for that leg of the trip were poor for visual flight rule aviation, and there was some question about whether or not we should even go. The weather forecast for the remote area where we were headed consisted of looking at the sky at the lodge, comparing what you saw with the current report from the coastal fishing village of Nain three hundred kilometers to the north and then guessing what it might be doing in between. Marco thought it would be okay, and if not, we could always turn back.

It was only overcast and chilly when we took off, but once we were in the air and headed north, rain streaked the cockpit windows, wind buffeted the small plane and to stay under the low ceiling we hugged the deck close enough not only to clearly see migrating caribou, but all but count the points on their antlers. But Marco exuded an air of confidence that was contagious, and I inherently trust bush pilots anyway on the premise that they know what they're doing and are no more eager to die than I am. On the other hand, I can still involuntarily pucker the upholstery when the ground seems to be getting too close.

After several hours in the air, Marco landed smoothly on a small lake and put us ashore near the inlet of a river with an unpronounceable Innu name. While the four of us set up camp in a light but steady rain, Marco grabbed a fly rod and trotted over to the mouth of the river, where he quickly landed and killed five or six large char. These fish are a delicacy, and in the normal course of things, one of them would become dinner, while the rest would enter the regional subsistence economy as currency, gifts or bribes. Before Marco took off, he squinted meaningfully at the lowering gray sky and said he'd be back to pick us up in a couple of days—weather permitting. Of course "weather permitting" is the caveat that accompanies all plans in the far north and that gives you a specific twinge of loneliness as you watch the plane bank out of sight.

Within a few hours the storm had socked in like it was there to stay, with rain and a stiff, chilly breeze coming steadily out of the northeast, straight off the north Atlantic. (The air may or may not have smelled salty, but I imagined it did.) We'd set up the wall tent behind a copse of black spruce trees that acted as a windbreak and had the dry sleeping bags stashed safely inside. The food boxes were roped up into a tree out of reach of bears, and Robin and Jimmy had rigged an upwind tarp to a tripod of spruce poles to shelter the campfire from the rain. There was a pot of coffee on.

We had a few days' worth of groceries, a basic kitchen kit, assorted tarps, a hatchet, spare coils of rope, a chain saw for firewood, a handful of 12-gauge shells and an ancient Russian-made shotgun that looked like it would be equally lethal at either end. We'd found the skull of a large caribou near the beach and were using the antlers as a convenient rod rack.

The surrounding countryside was rolling hills with scattered stands of stubby black spruce and a few tall, feathery tamaracks set in mostly open ground. The tight ground cover was a preview of Arctic tundra not far from the northern tree line, which isn't a line at all, but a ragged edge where one kind of habitat gradually gives way to another until the northernmost wins. It may not have been literally true, but there was the feeling that we were about as far into the remaining North American wilderness as you could get without being in danger of coming out the other side: relatively cozy and safe from anything short of an extinction-level event.

Over at the river—a quarter-mile walk from camp over a low hill—countless char had nosed up into the first two sets of rapids above the lake, where they were hungrily feeding on a sputtering but often heavy hatch of size 14 mayflies. The river is wide there and from the top of that rise you could see that literally hundreds of fish were working from bank to bank. This is exactly what you hope for (but don't quite dare to expect) when you've flown three-quarters of the way across North America in order to wet a line.

Over the next few days we learned that this hatch would come off more or less predictably between around noon and six o'clock. There were times when the water was fuzzy with mayfly wings and the char would happily take a parachute dry fly. When the hatch slowed down a little, they preferred a size 14 nymph swung down and across the current wet-fly–style. The char ran anywhere from three to six or seven pounds, not to mention the ones that spooled off fly line and backing, parked out in the main current and stayed there, eventually either breaking off your fly or sending back a straightened hook. With the usual variations, this would go on like clockwork for no less than six hours a day.

The lodge does fly parties in here now and then, usually just for the day, but Robin said the fishing had always been a much more plodding affair with streamers or deeply sunk nymphs and that he'd never seen a blanket hatch like this. Then again, they'd always flown in on the kind of bright, calm, sunny days that are often better for flying than for fishing, while the hatch was almost surely brought on by the increasingly skanky weather that would normally have made the river inaccessible. It was just dumb luck that allowed us to get in there under the storm and stumble into better fishing than anyone expected.

The char weren't on the redds yet, but that far north the fall spawn was already in the air in mid-August, and the male fish were colored up beautifully with greenish bronze backs shading through bright red spots to fire-engine-red bellies. The pectoral, caudal and anal fins were translucent reddish orange with the same brilliant white leading edge you'll see on a brook trout. The fish were wide-shouldered and beefy, with tails that were forked, oversized and designed for speed. Arctic char are notorious for having different coloration in every watershed where they're found, but these were far and away the brightest ones I'd ever seen.

C.D. decided to paint a portrait of an especially handsome five-pounder he'd killed. I had assumed the weather was too crappy for plein-air painting, but he worked under a neat spruce pole and plastic tarp lean-to he and Jimmy built to block the wind and rain. He said it worked fine except that by the time he finished, a thousand blackflies had joined him in the shelter. The painting was lovely and the fish itself was delicious, breaded lightly in cornmeal and fried in bacon grease.

By the evening of the second day, the storm had developed an air of permanence, and it became clear that Marco wouldn't be flying in to get us in the morning as planned. Just to be sure, Robin called the lodge on a satellite phone and told him not to come. He said he didn't intend to.

Robin made the same call on day three, but later learned that Marco had tried to get to the river anyway because he thought Robin was being overly cautious—which is actually not a bad trait in this country. Subsequent calls told us that Marco ran into weather halfway there and had to make an emergency landing on a small, nameless lake. The squall had hit so suddenly that he didn't even have time to make the usual pass over the water where he planned to land to make sure there were no protruding rocks or floating logs that he could run into. He thought he'd have to spend the night in the plane, but then a small break in the clouds let him take off again and just make it back to a hot meal and a dry bed at the lodge by dark. When I asked why he'd even tried, Robin said that Marco just enjoyed being right, especially when it meant that he, Robin, was wrong. He said this was nothing serious, just the usual male strutting.

By then we had settled in nicely. In hindsight, this would be a little adventure that would be tempting to overdramatize in the retelling, but there's something commonplace about day-to-day life in camp that keeps that from occurring to you at the time. There were meals to be cooked, dishes to be washed, firewood to be cut and the constant tending of the fire itself. Robin and C.D. were both good storytellers, and Jimmy turned out to be a rare good-natured man of few words. These are the only two kinds of people you want to camp with.

A high point came when I revealed that I knew the secret recipe for traditional eggshell coffee, which is simply to put the breakfast eggshells in the pot along with the boiling grounds. That little bit of dissolved egg white enriches the coffee so subtly that the difference could be imaginary, but everyone I know claims to be able to taste it. After that, I was put in charge of the morning coffee, as if the eggshells had to be placed just so or it wouldn't work.

It rained and blew constantly, sometimes hard, sometimes more lightly. Two or three times it stopped raining altogether for fifteen or twenty minutes at a time, but the breeze stayed steady and the ceiling was so low that it seemed almost possible to reach up and touch the clouds with the tip of your nine-foot fly rod. We lived in chest waders and rain slickers and stayed as dry as possible under the circumstances (that is, systemically damp, but somewhere short of soaking wet). A young black bear peeked into camp one morning, but he seemed more wary than curious and there were lots of low-bush blueberries for him to eat, so, as far as we know, he never came back.

We cooked on smoky fires started with chain-saw gas, and as the only freestanding warmth within a hundred kilometers in any direction, the fire itself took on near-religious significance. Otherwise we simply talked, slept, ate and headed out to fish as if it were a job—but the kind of job where you whistle as you walk to work. C.D. did another painting—a somber landscape—and on two separate mornings he walked down to the lake to bathe and shave in the cold water. Robin said that anyone who shaved in camp was a true sporting gentleman. I assumed that was a compliment.

By the end of the second day we had already caught as many big, wild fish as any sane man needs to catch, but at its best the fishing was just short of taking candy from a baby, so of course we kept at it. The best fishing is usually done with no motive other than curiosity, and on those rare trips when your curiosity is completely satisfied, you can begin to feel a little untethered. On the other hand, we wanted to see how long this could possibly go on. There was no danger of boredom, but we did have the leisure to try several different flies out of curiosity. All of them worked to some degree, and I discovered that if you swung a weighted, hot-pink streamer through the rising char, you could pick up the occasional ten- or twelve-pound lake trout.

We tried some different water, and one day C.D. and Jimmy hiked far upriver, but there seemed to be fewer fish the farther you got from the inlet, so we always ended up back at the same few spots near camp. After a while the rusty blackbirds that were feeding on mayflies plucked from bankside currents got so used to us they'd perch boldly within arm's reach, although the harlequin ducks continued to keep their distance. I believe that we each privately asked ourselves the unanswerable question—How much is enough?—and felt fortunate to even have it come up.

Eventually the food began to run low, but that didn't seem especially dire since we'd already eaten several meals of fish (each more luscious than the last) and figured we could always eat more. That wasn't so much a certainty as just the overconfidence that comes too easily from days of good fishing. But then the fishing only got better as the weather got worse. Our only worry was that we were running dangerously short of coffee and would soon have to start rationing.

Marco finally picked us up on the fifth morning, when the storm began to clear and there was a streak of actual blue sky on the eastern horizon. He buzzed the camp with his pontoons at treetop level while we were eating a breakfast consisting of the last of the coffee and packets of instant oatmeal that Robin said had been in the bottom of the food box for the last three or four years.

The prospect of a hot shower, dry clothes and a little mothering from Frances back at the lodge was appealing, but C.D. and I had already agreed that although there'd been the vague sense that we needed to be res-

cued, there was no real urge to leave. We'd been technically stranded, but the feeling was more that we'd found
the perfect hiding place and were in no rush to be found.
I thought of the old Irish toast: "May you be in heaven a
few days before the devil knows you're dead."

The next time I gave much thought to airlines and ter-
rorism was a few days later on the flight from the lodge
back to Wabush. Acting on week-old, secondhand information, I had dutifully stashed my toothpaste and mosquito repellent in my checked baggage, right on top so it
would be easy to get to if it was confiscated. No one knew
quite what to expect, and the evening before at the lodge,
two fishermen were unsure if they'd be allowed to fly with
an eighty-dollar bottle of scotch, so they drank it, which
seemed like a reasonable precaution.

The flight back was slow and bumpy with a strong
headwind, and at the dock in Wabush, Marco announced
that he'd landed with only five gallons of gas left in the
tank, barely enough to taxi in. There are pilots who would
have kept that information to themselves.

As it turned out, security at Wabush was a relative
breeze, partly because it's a tiny airport with a single de-
parture gate and not many passengers, but also because,
as a visiting fisherman once famously said, "Canadians
are just like Americans, except they're *nice.*" Still, there
was the Orwellian vision of government agents pawing
through your personal belongings and reading the labels
on your prescription medication, although at least at the
airport you're there to witness it. Not so with your mail,

e-mail, telephone and bank accounts or with the count-less, spooky security cameras that are trained on us daily. Which is to say, civilization isn't all bad, but a sudden re-entry can be a shock to the system.

Outside the terminal it was raining steadily again and the wind was blowing at about thirty miles an hour, which meant another turbulent flight south to Montreal. I was waiting to board the same plane as the two guys who'd polished off the scotch the night before. They both looked a little green and I was hoping I wouldn't have to sit next to them.

16. Nebraska

Ed Engle and I were fishing some prairie lakes in the northern Nebraska Sandhills, and our seasonal timing was off by a couple of weeks, which every fisherman will immediately recognize as a handicap. The best time to fish these shallow, marshy lakes is in the spring when the water is just warm enough for the largemouth bass to be starting to spawn—or at least thinking about it seriously—but still just chilly enough for the cool-water-loving northern pike to be actively feeding during the day: a moving window of water temperature that in some years only stays completely open for two or three weeks.

There are other variables, as well as the usual imponderables that always crop up in fishing, but as a general rule, you'll probably do okay if you can hit a week with water temperatures in the low to mid sixties. There's a little elbow room, since these lakes vary in size from about fifty acres to almost eight hundred and can warm up earlier or later according to their size, depth, weed growth and the number and flow of the springs that feed them. But even if you know which lake is which, that usually doesn't amount to more than an extra week or two of wiggle room.

This year the water had warmed unseasonably early, so by the time Ed and I arrived in the last week of May, the weather and the fish had both begun to ease into a pattern more typical of the summer doldrums. A fisherman will tell you that fish often "sulk" during hot days: a euphemism meaning that they may bite in rare moments of weakness or excitability, but they're not really on the feed. It's a way of laying the blame for poor fishing on the fish themselves, as if they'd signed contracts agreeing to be caught.

Middays that week were sunny and hot, and the wind was often blowing hard enough that launching my fourteen-foot aluminum johnboat with twelve inches of freeboard took a degree of either courage or foolhardiness. (Frankly this wind was a pain in the ass, although when it would die for a half hour or so, the heat would become suffocating and you'd immediately want it back again.) On the windiest days it was possible to envy the oceangoing bass boats you sometimes see on the bigger lakes: the ones with dual-axle trailers, metal flake paint jobs, upholstered swivel seats and hundred-pound-thrust trolling motors.

You see the widest imaginable assortment of boats on these lakes, from those that obviously cost as much as the new trucks towing them to some that don't really look like they'd float. I like to think that mine is near the

middle in terms of seaworthiness, but given the apprais-
ing glances from some of the more serious bass types, it
could be slightly toward the low end. These sidelong looks
not only include the craft, but the vehicles towing them
and the people who own them. They nonverbally commu-
nicate a wealth of information, since the only thing that
will tell you more about a fisherman than his boat is how
he treats his dog.

The fishing was so slow most days that we quickly fell into a program of going out in the cooler, calmer
mornings, lounging around our little rented cabin at the
nearby Big Alkali Fish Camp during midday, and then going out again in the evenings when, for an hour and a
half or so, the wind would drop, the light would slant, the
air would cool, and large, hungry bass would move into
the weedy shallows to feed. Night fishing could have been
excellent, but one of the few rules here is that you have
to be off the water by dark. A ranger we'd met had told us
that he, at least, wasn't a real stickler about it, but that if
you were still out on a lake after sunset you had better be
making an obvious move toward the boat ramp. We took
that as license to push it by half an hour to forty-five minutes, but no more.

As Ed pointed out in his optimistic way, the long
fishless days only made the witching hours in the evenings
more glorious. As for those dead afternoons, I've come to
think that getting bored only means you've failed to master the fine art of doing nothing when there's nothing to
be done: a skill you can learn from any house cat.

Actually, Ed and I hadn't even planned to go out
there this year, but then Jeri Ballard, who has run the
camp for the last twenty-some seasons, called to say that

the State of Nebraska was pulling the lease on the camp and closing it down, so we decided on the spot to make a valedictory trip.

We'd discovered the place by accident a decade ago while on one of those open-ended fishing trips to explore the lakes on the nearby Valentine National Wildlife Refuge. In the course of looking for a place to camp, we pulled off the state highway at a weathered sign, crossed a cattle guard and rumbled half a mile down a sand and gravel road pocked with potholes. We ended up in an oasislike grove of mature hardwoods alive with bird songs and shading some ramshackle cabins. We ended up splitting twenty-four bucks a night for a week in a cramped cabin with electricity, a rudimentary kitchen, a cold-water tap and a perfectly good two-hole outhouse in back.

We've done exactly the same thing now for nine out of the last ten years because the place was irresistible. It was cheap, comfortable as an old shoe, a scant fifteen miles on good roads from the refuge lakes, and Jeri was like everyone's favorite aunt from the farm as well as an up-to-the-minute repository of accurate fishing news.

We began the process of fine-tuning that characterizes any regular trip. In the beginning we were car-topping the boat—which I liked for its informality and ease of parking—but then one fall I hurt my back cutting firewood and my doctor told me my days of lifting and carrying hundred-fifty-pound boats were over. "Just get a trailer," he said. But this is not an insensitive man, and when he noticed my disappointment, he added, "Look, you just don't want to reinjure your back. You're actually in excellent shape for a man your age" (which is sort of like saying "You don't sweat much for a fat broad").

The trailer somehow nullified some Spartan principle and was followed in quick succession by a trolling motor with thirty-six-pound thrust, a pair of batteries (a big bruiser and a smaller spare), a battery charger and a new set of ash oars called Smokers. This amounted to over a thousand dollars' worth of accoutrements for a hundred-dollar used boat, but it seemed unavoidable.

We also quickly got into the habit of bringing more than enough provisions for a week because the nearest real grocery store was a sixty-mile round-trip from the camp. You could pick up a few odds and ends at the camp store, but they sold mostly soft drinks, potato chips and that brand of hot dogs that swell when you cook them, a sight gruesome enough to cost you your appetite.

We soon ended up with a regular cabin reserved for the same week every spring and we always laughed at Jeri's signs instructing fishermen not to pour grease down the drain or charge their trolling batteries on the rug, but of course we always did as we were told. By the time you read this, the state will have bulldozed the place and re-built it with shiny new (and more expensive) cabins and a store that will be run not by the easygoing Ballard family, but by a state employee who may or may not consider this a plum assignment. It will never be the same, but in another twenty or thirty years the place might begin to redevelop some character. You can never be sure, but somehow I doubt we'll ever go back.

We didn't bother checking on the fishing conditions because this would be our last trip to the place and it was more of a sentimental journey than an actual fishing trip, but that's not to say that we drove all the way out there just to pout. It's now possible to wear out a way of life in less than a lifetime and you can get either angry or morose as the world you've learned to live in becomes unrecognizable, but it won't stop or even slow the process. And anyway, although gazing at the past is pleasant enough, it can cause you to back into the future ass-first, which I don't recommend.

Ed and I are both primarily trout guys, but there's something about fly fishing for largemouth bass and pike that we just can't leave alone. You can certainly spend an inordinate amount of money on this kind of fishing, but that's not quite the requirement it is in trout fishing and in fact a workmanlike simplicity is still admired. It's also more unpredictably rough-and-tumble than most trout fishing, and there's an ambience about the whole enterprise that trips some old, well-worn synapses from childhood. It's hard to pin that last element down, but as Ed said, the camp is straight out of the 1950s, and we fish from a boat that could easily have belonged to either of our fathers. That can't be entirely coincidental.

As I said, the difference is hard to explain, but I'm one of those who often gets music stuck in my head while fishing—pleasantly or otherwise. When I'm trout fishing, it's likely to be "Treetop Flyer" by Steve Stills or even half-remembered snatches of Vivaldi's *Four Seasons*. When I'm bass or pike fishing, it's more likely to be "I Love to Go Swimmin' with Bowlegged Women."

As usual when the fishing is slow but not completely off, there were some excellent moments. Most of our bass were caught on floating deer-hair bugs with weed guards and most of the strikes were spectacularly visual, with the fly going down in a swirl that looks like a flushing toilet, as more than one fishing writer has so eloquently described it. But then my biggest bass ate the fly with a miniature dimple worthy of a four-inch bluegill. In fact, that's what I thought it was until I noticed that the entire size 4 bug had disappeared from the surface. When I finally came to my senses and set the hook, all hell briefly broke loose. Landing a large bass on a fly rod in thick bulrushes is exciting as hell, but not particularly pretty.

Most of the few pike we got ate heavily weighted Eelworm–style streamers in deeper water, but then one evening on Dewey Lake I'd switched to a floating deer-hair frog hoping for a bass in the last of the light and ended up hooking a pike I couldn't land.

The fish took in one of those long, rushing strikes that brought him partly out of the water, and Ed and I both saw enough of him to comprehend that this was a very big pike. The usual recipe for landing an extremely large fish on a fly rod is that the fisherman does everything right, while the fish does at least one little thing wrong. In this case there was a moment when it could have gone either way, but I'd hooked the fish within inches of a thick stand of flooded reeds, and when he ran for the cover, he gave me a rope burn on the fingers that were holding my fly line. Then he neatly tied me off in the stalks and threw the barbless hook. I may have howled out loud from disappointment or I may have suppressed it. I don't remember, and Ed was too polite to say anything beyond, "Aw, too bad, man."

There's a particular etiquette to fishing when the sweet spot is so brief. The fisherman stands in the bow while the boatman works either the oars or the pole, depending on the density of the cover. When a fish is hooked, there are times when the boatman just sits back and watches the fun and other times when he must act quickly and plays an integral part in fighting and landing the thing. You've spent the day exploring or back at cabin 7 reading, watching orchard orioles and jabbering in a kind of caffeine-induced stream of consciousness, but now you're on the water and between hearing the first sploosh back in the weeds that's obviously a fish of some size and dark, you have a scant two hours at best.

The rules are unspoken, but strictly adhered to: You relinquish the rod based on how well the fish are biting, how long they'll continue to bite and when the conditions will change. Not that you actually know any of that, but still . . . This amounts to time spent casting when the fishing is slow to the number of fish caught or strikes missed when it's hot. We've never bothered to discuss it, and as far as I know, neither of us has ever felt cheated by anything but our own dumb luck.

One day we got a tip from a friendly young Fish and Wildlife guy on a secret but still public bass lake a hundred miles away and took the long side trip to avoid killing another afternoon. We were driving straight east within a stone's throw of the South Dakota border when we passed a billboard that said WELCOME TO THE MIDDLE OF NOWHERE. A little farther on we stopped in the little town of Ainsworth for gas and found the place festooned with American flags because it was Memorial Day, which I'd somehow forgotten.

I'll admit that my heart gripped a little at the sight. I'm capable of being so cynical about such things that I sometimes even annoy myself, but there is simply nothing more poignantly and defiantly festive than that flag on that day in this country in these times. Of course the pang was characteristically selfish: a moment of regret that I'd spent so much of my youth being entirely too hip to appreciate anything this homespun and heartfelt.

At the gas station we got a couple of those looks that aren't at all unfriendly, but simply register the presence of someone clearly not from around there. I've been told that I wear my politics on my sleeve and can be spotted a mile away, but I think it's more of a lingering cultural aura that says, Here is a man who functions in society at a fairly high level, but who nonetheless did not escape the 1960s entirely unscathed.

But then virtually everywhere I've been in rural America, you get the benefit of the doubt unless you demonstrate otherwise, and politeness is automatically returned in kind, so if you say "please" and "thank you" and maybe hold a door for a lady, you're speaking the regional dialect. There's also the universal symbolism of two guys in a pickup truck towing a bass boat, which most take to mean that you can't be all bad. Ed and I may not be straight out of Norman Rockwell, but it's been decades since anyone asked us if we were hippies or werewolves.

The young ranger's directions were impeccable, and we could see what he meant about the lake. It was public and there was even a small brown sign announcing the fact, but it was effectively in the middle of nowhere, as the highway sign said, and you could miss it even if you knew it was there. In fact, I would have missed it if Ed hadn't pointed and said, "I think that's it." I'd been distracted by a large wind farm on a nearby ridge that would produce cheap, clean, sustainable energy but also act as a meat grinder for migratory birds.

Between a wind so strong and hot it felt like you were standing in the door of a blast furnace and a thick algae bloom that turned the lake to pea soup, the fishing was a complete bust, but the obscure little wildlife management area was a riot of bird life. I'll spare you the complete list (except for the dickcissels because I like the name), but I *will* say that in the area refuges surrounding many of these Sandhill lakes a diligent and lucky birder could see as many as two hundred seventy different species of bird, many of which nest there. In fact, if you're wading around in the marsh to fish, you have to walk on eggshells to avoid literally walking on eggshells.

The continuous racket was incredible. Shorebirds in mating season seldom shut up, and killdeer in particular live in a perpetual state of hysteria about their territories. I remembered nature writer Annie Dillard once saying that as pretty as we think bird songs are, their human equivalent would be to scream "Mine!" at the top of your lungs over and over again.

Just as Ed and I were leaving to get what turned out be among the top five steak dinners of my life up in the town of Valentine, a pair of fishermen pulled in and asked through the window of their pickup how we'd done. I said the fishing sucked, but it was a nice place if you liked to watch birds. The driver guffawed and slapped his knee, as if the idea of a bass fisherman who was also a bird watcher was a real hoot.

17. Umpqua

Vince and I had been told that the North Umpqua in western Oregon was a difficult steelhead river, although, come to think of it, I don't think either of us has ever heard of an *easy* steelhead river. Anyway, when we went out there in March to try to catch the winter run, we hedged our bet by hiring a guide. His name was Bob Burruss, and when we talked on the phone a month or so earlier, I said I wanted him to show us around the first day so we could fish on our own for the rest of the week. He said, "Yeah, that's a good idea."

I think it really *is* a good idea. Even if you're a smart and observant fisherman who doesn't need professional hand-holding, it can still take what seems like forever to figure out the easiest fraction of what a good local guide can show you in a day. And if you're like me, you'll pick up even that little bit so late in the trip that you barely have any time left to use it.

First thing Monday morning Bob handed us photocopied maps of the river's thirty-some miles of roadside fly fishing–only water. Throughout the day he keyed the good pools and runs to mile markers, turnouts and other prominent landmarks as we scribbled notes and drew arrows on our maps. Of course these sketches were dashed off in improvised shorthand, often in a moving car, so later some were undecipherable, but even then we learned the dozen or so pools we'd fished, plus enough others to last at least a week.

Bob is a retired high school football coach, and he has the tightly wound enthusiasm you might remember from those days. At first I thought he was a little too frenetic, firing more information at you than you could possibly absorb, but it quickly became obvious that this came from a peculiar combination of knowledge and generosity. It was the habit of a Coach with a capital *C* accustomed to whipping recalcitrant teenagers into shape: the polar opposite of a guide who's just going through the motions.

And in fact, it was interesting how much of that rapid-fire instruction filtered back over the subsequent days when Vince and I were fishing on our own—as well as a burgeoning, if not entirely justified, sense of confidence that had rubbed off on us from the experience. At the end of that first fishless day, Bob suggested a good place to start the next morning, then shook our hands and said, "Okay boys, you've got the skills, now use 'em."

A lot of what we came away with that day was specific and nowhere near obvious. For instance, in one spot you'd want to swing your fly at a depth of no less than three feet along a short but steep shelf rock in mid-river. At another you'd want to fish the tailout of an almost indistinguishable tub in otherwise riffly water. Yet another run could be good if you were the first one to fish it in the morning. Otherwise, forget it. The stretch that used to be Zane Grey's favorite was worth fishing for sentimental reasons, and it could also still hold fish all these years later, although of course it would be nowhere near as good as it was back in the old days.

The North Umpqua is a brawling canyon river that's hard for a beginner to read because its basalt bedrock bottom is a maze of sudden slots, bumps, ridges, trenches and knobs formed by old lava flows and worn smooth by current. There are a few recognizable cast-and-step runs where you can get in at the top and shuffle down, but in many places the wading difficulties mean you have to fish entire runs from one or two precarious perches.

Bob showed us a technique for feeding mends into successive down-and-across-stream casts that would let you swing a fly through more water than you could reach with a conventional spey cast. (Unless you were a world champion caster, this was the only way to adequately fish some runs.) I'd heard about this, but like so many things in fishing that you only hear about, it makes no more than theoretical sense until you see someone do it well.

We'd been told that the wading was slippery and treacherous, but that turned out to be an understatement.

The bedrock bottom is not only startlingly uneven, but, as Trey Combs said in his book *Steelhead Fly Fishing*, the rocks are "polished ice-smooth from the fine grit of countless springs, and annually slimed with algae." It's been said that when you wade the North Umpqua you might as well just jump in the river first thing in the morning and get it over with. That's the standard joke, but then everyone we talked to pointedly asked if we had cleats and wading staffs, and they did it in that way fishermen have of lowering the voice and leveling the stare that says, I'm not joshing now; this is serious shit. This is a river you could drown in.

We had brought both and we used them, but I'm so inexperienced with strap-on cleats that they're as likely to trip me up as they are to help me grip the slick bottom. I also had the disadvantage of following two much larger guys. Bob and Vince are both strong, athletically built two-hundred-plus-pounders, while I'm a little clumsy and weigh one hundred sixty soaking wet, as they say. (Back in my manual-labor days, they used to say, "A good big man is better than a good *little* man.") I quickly learned to be skeptical when one of them said, "You can cross easily right there." We learned the local trick of picking our way out to convenient casting perches by following the faint cleat marks left by more experienced fishermen, but in some spots these turned out to be the trails of some pretty adventurous waders.

I only went in twice, and only one of those was your classic ass-over-teakettle dunk in fast current that left me soaked from beard to socks. I remember that one moment of pure, primitive panic when I was in up to my chin, legs tangled in my wading staff, couldn't get my cleats under me and couldn't grab the greasy rocks that passed too quickly as I washed downstream toward white water. In peripheral vision I registered Vince coming for me as fast as he could wade, but it was pretty clear to both of us that he wouldn't make it.

My next recollection is of wallowing toward the bank under partial control and realizing I was holding onto my spey rod so tightly I expected to find a handprint embossed in the cork grip. It was a feeling I've experienced a few other times in my life: once while trying to climb ice in ill-fitting Army surplus crampons, two or three times in airplanes, once in a hospital and so on. In each case, nothing had flashed before my eyes and there was no epiphany to try to remember and learn from; I'd been just another drowning mammal.

I wrung myself out as well as possible and fished on for a while after that, but I must have looked as cold as I was because Vince finally said, "Okay, you're going back to the motel to get into some dry clothes." I thought about arguing in order to seem brave, but I didn't.

Naturally conditions on the river that week weren't right. (I say naturally because I've yet to go steelheading and have someone say, "Everything is perfect; you couldn't have picked a better time.") But even though the sky was too clear, the weather a bit too warm and the flow too low for March, the water temperature was right and fish were moving upstream. Steelhead are never easy to catch and these seemed harder than usual, but at least they were there. If you came to doubt that after hours of casting, you could drive to the bottom of the fly-only water and watch them vaulting a pretty waterfall at the approximate rate of a fish every thirty seconds.

We talked to some other fishermen, who allowed as how things were slow. They said fish were beginning to dribble in, but the main run hadn't arrived yet. Maybe if the sky clouded up, the fish that were there would get a little more aggressive. Maybe it would rain soon and bump the river up, bringing in more steelhead. Maybe the fishing would be better in a couple more weeks. Two locals said they'd been out once or twice when time had permitted, but they were waiting for things to improve a little more before they'd ditch work to hit it hard. As tourists on something resembling a schedule, we didn't have that luxury.

I remembered a guy we'd met on the Salmon River in Idaho the first week of the previous October. He was our neighbor in the campground, and we met when he warned us to keep our camp stove clean and our food stowed because a black bear had been sniffing around the last few nights. We said we'd be there for the week. He said he'd be there for the month of October and maybe part of November, depending on when the fishing got good. He struck me as the blue-collar version of Charles Ritz, the Ritz Hotel heir, who once said he refused to accept any invitation to go salmon fishing for less than a month because even on the best rivers at the best times of year, that's how long it could take to hit it right.

We'd see this guy on the river every once in a while, sometimes fishing, but more often driving around with his old yellow Lab and a thermos of coffee on the seat beside him, jawing with other fishermen. Back at camp, we'd exchange a few polite words, but the guy spent most of his evenings in a lawn chair peacefully staring into his fire. He wasn't at all unfriendly, just self-contained: the very picture of a man with all the time in the world. He wasn't around when we broke camp at the end of the week, so we didn't get to say goodbye, but we added what was left of our seasoned elm firewood to his own pile of pine, figuring he'd know where it came from.

It has become obvious that getting into fly fishing for steelhead is like taking a vow of voluntary poverty. You know that even if you eventually get very good at it (not likely for someone who lives as far from steelhead water as I do), the good days will be few and far between and they'll be measured by a different standard than the one we lifelong trout fishers are used to. Even if you wait it out to the bitter end, the favorable pounds-of-fish-per-hours-of-casting ratio some fishermen aspire to just doesn't pan out with sea-run fish.

This can keep you away from it for a long time, but eventually you may tumble out of curiosity. The experience is a little like your first sip of Dad's coffee as a curious ten-year-old: it's bitter and astringent and Dad grins as your face puckers, but then all too soon it becomes an acquired taste you can't live without. You fish as if working through each run smoothly and methodically were your only goal and you do it at a relaxed and steady pace, taking breaks when your concentration begins to wilt or when you fall in the river and have to go back to the motel to dry out. I've heard it said by extreme types that you can't fish for steelhead casually, but actually that's the only way I *can* do it.

Of course there's no point to deep thinking about fishing while you're actually fishing. In the last hours of a day without a strike, you're more likely to remember the old definition of a fisherman as "a jerk on one end of a line waiting for a jerk on the other end." You may now and then wonder what the hell you're doing there, although you can't quite think of anywhere else you'd rather be. More likely, the part of your mind that isn't absorbed in watching your fly line may wade to shore and stand in the chilly spruce forest listening for winter birds, not hoping for anything more remarkable than a gray jay, a Clark's nutcracker, a raven or a chickadee. Apparently this is a pleasure that's unavailable to your average fun hog. As someone once asked, "How can you just *stand* out there all day?"

Later, on the way to the local joint where you'll get an enormous lumberjack special slathered in "Uncle So-and-so's secret sauce," it might occur to you that in a more authentic world, a couple of fishless days in a row would mean you'd be in for a long, hungry night. But then you pull in at the sign of the fat, smiling cartoon beaver wearing a logger's wide-brimmed hard hat and the thought dissolves. The food isn't especially good, but there's lots of it and you're hungry as a wolf. Early the next morning at the motel, after an inordinately long stay in the toilet, Vince announces, "I think I've discovered the secret of the secret sauce." And life goes on.

Vince and I did each eventually land a steelhead. Mine came from a spot Bob had showed us on that first day. It was just a shallow dish in fast water that I'd have walked by without a second glance, but Bob had pointed out how it was the first place a steelhead could stop and catch its breath after running up an eighth of a mile of steep riffle, so it often held fish. It was a spot known to some, but not enough to have a trail of cleat marks leading to the obvious casting rock.

The fish ate one of the flies Bill Black had given us that morning when we ran into him over breakfast in town. (Bill is a well-known local steelheader who makes a living selling flies, so you don't just take the fly to be polite, you also fish it.) These things were tied in the style that's getting popular now, with a cone head and a single hook dropped two and a half inches behind the eye on limp backing material. Their advantage is that they're good-sized flies, but with short-shanked hooks that are harder for a fish to throw, and of course they wiggle. (In the long history of fishing lures, things that wiggle have always been considered superior to things that don't.) I forget now exactly what these things are called—Intruders or Penetrators or something like that. I try to stay abreast of broad trends in the sport, but I guess I missed the moment when steelhead flies began to look and sound like sex toys.

The fish took with one of those slow, current-speed pulls that could be your fly hanging on a rock but isn't. Later, Vince said that when the fish felt the hook and jumped, the look of surprise on my face was profound, but I played and landed it expertly, which is to say, I didn't totally panic or fall in the river. It turned out to be a bright, wild fourteen-pound hen, all silver with just a blush of pink on the gill covers and still sporting the adipose fin that's clipped off on hatchery fish. She was fresh enough that she could still have had sea lice, but I didn't think to look until after I'd released her. As usual, it all happened so fast.

18. The Meeting

My friend was half an hour late to go fishing, so when the phone rang, I knew it was him. The plan had been for him to slip out of work early so we could run up to a nearby tailwater for the afternoon and see what the trout were doing. Of course we thought we already knew what they'd be doing, since the spring blue-winged olive mayfly hatch was on and it was the kind of cold, stormy winter-throwback day those bugs are known to like.

 I was thinking car trouble, but my friend said no, he was "stuck in a meeting," and then paused long enough for that phrase to sink in. He understands that I've been self-employed for so long now that it takes a conscious effort to wrap my mind around that kind of corporate reality.

His voice had the hollow, liquid ring you get from a cell phone, which caused me to picture the conference room as an enormous, damp rain barrel. I told him it was okay and drove up to the river, sincerely hoping that the meeting went well enough to justify missing an afternoon of fishing, but doubting it would. I've been to only a handful of meetings in my life. More than half of them quickly degenerated into droning nonsense, and the few that didn't would have gone just fine without me.

It was cold and bitter on the river, as I expected. On the short drive up there from my house, you gain 2,300-some feet in elevation, lose as much as twenty degrees in temperature, and the light drizzle at home turns to the sleet-snow hybrid known locally as "snoosh." These cold early-April storms in the Rocky Mountains can have a raw edge that outdoes anything in midwinter, if only because the humidity tends to be higher and because it's spring, for Pete's sake, and you can't help thinking it should at least be above freezing by afternoon. On the other hand, the fish seem to like it, and as the fish go, so goes the fisherman.

When you're on a popular roadside river, you never plan on fishing any particular spot in order to avoid being utterly disappointed if there's another fisherman already there. Instead you try to stay loose and inventive, checking the turnouts for cars, scanning the water for fishermen and just generally aiming for a quick lay of the land. If the river is crowded, you immediately write off the obvious pools and begin checking out the potholes and stretches of interesting pocket water in between or, in a pinch, the long riffles that conceal a few fishy tubs that you imagine not just anyone knows about. There are days when that's a little annoying, but in fact it's this pacifist strategy of avoiding competition that has led you—sometimes in near desperation—to some of the coolest little hidden spots you know.

But things were looking weirdly vacant that afternoon. There was no one parked at the Dead Elk turnout: the first one you come to and virtually everyone's favorite spot on that stretch of river. Same for the Green Bridge, Whispering Pines, and so on down the canyon. I drove almost a mile downriver, past some of the best water, and there wasn't a soul anywhere, so I pulled off to think this over. Having a normally crowded river all to yourself is the kind of thing that *does* sometimes happen, but my native cynicism always makes me question my luck. Maybe a tanker truck full of toxic waste crashed into the river and all the fish are dead. I'm the only fisherman in two counties who doesn't know about it because I haven't looked at a newspaper in two weeks in the interest of mental health.

I turned around and parked up at the Forest Service sign, where I took the last of my still-warm coffee and ambled over to look at the water. There's a long pool full of fish there where, during even a sparse hatch, you can easily see trout rising and violet-green swallows wheeling over the water. It was too early in the season for the swallows, but there were no rings on the water from feeding fish either, so apparently the hatch wasn't on. There were also no crippled mayflies or shed nymphal shucks in the bankside slicks, so either the hatch hadn't happened yet, or it had, but it was too thin to leave any sign. As someone could be saying in my friend's meeting at that very moment, "There's insufficient data to make a determination at this time."

That took all of three or four minutes, during which my ears and fingers started to sting and my coffee went from lukewarm to stone-cold. The wind wasn't much more than a breeze, but to paraphrase Lou Rawls, it felt like razor blades blowing down the river.

I've noticed that when I fish alone the usual machismo disengages to some degree. That is, I fish slower, wade shallower, and spend more time looking at birds and scenery. My friends don't exactly egg me on, but when I'm in their company, I tend to egg *myself* on. Anyway, with nothing to prove, I wasn't out to prove anything, and to cover my back later I could always say I'd gone up to the river and "not much was going on," never quite mentioning that I hadn't even strung up a rod. But then without giving it any more thought, I bundled up and went fishing. Call it momentum.

Within fifteen minutes on the water I was uncomfortably cold. I was wearing eleven separate pieces of clothing—everything I'd brought—plus fingerless gloves and the insulated Elmer Fudd hat with the fuzzy earflaps that I consider the height of foul-weather sporting fashion. Naturally, I'd buggered up my leader the last time out and hadn't bothered to repair it at home (at my leisure and with warm hands) so by the time I'd tied on a new 5X wear section, a 6X tippet, a size 18 Blue-winged Olive nymph and a small twist of lead, my fingers were dead numb. The fly choice was just my best guess based on the expected hatch, but I hoped it was right more fervently than usual because cutting it off and tying on a new one with fingers I couldn't feel would be a production.

I'll guess that the flies never quite came off that day because of the cold air, but that the mayfly nymphs were getting impatiently active under the surface. Once I waded into the river, I began to spot trout holding in a few feet of water on the inside of the main current. They were suspended off the bottom and noodling from side to side, busily taking nymphs. If the angle was right, I could sometimes see the white winks of their mouths opening to eat bugs. This is the lovely sight that tells a fly fisher he's in the game as long as he doesn't screw it up.

I caught three of the first five trout I cast to, and then tried a few drifts farther out toward the main channel where there were no fish, or they didn't like the fly, or the drift was bad, or the fly wasn't deep enough, or any of the dozens of other things that can make a negative difference. Okay, fair enough. The extra wet line on the longer casts was freezing in the guides anyway, and there were feeding trout virtually at my feet.

I moved on upstream in a slow-motion stalk so as not to spook fish before I could spot them, although of course I spooked a few anyway, including a rare eighteen- or nineteen-inch rainbow that would have been fun to try to land. There were trout feeding confidently in every spot where you'd expect to find them, suggesting that I not only had the river to myself at the moment, but that no one had fished through ahead of me anytime recently.

Once again I wondered about that. The water was clear, the flow was good, the hatch was widely known to be on, and there are plenty of locals who fish the river almost daily, including any number of tough customers who wouldn't be scared off by a little cold spring weather. So where the hell was everyone?

About then a guy came driving down the canyon road in a little red sedan. He slowed when he saw me and coasted by, giving me the now-universal blank stare we've all learned from watching too much television. If he was a fisherman, he was wondering how I was doing. If not, he was asking himself, Who's the moron in the dopey hat? I waved on general principle, but for all the response I got, I might as well have been a five-second film clip on the evening news. Not a fisherman, I decided; a fisherman would have waved back.

I had managed to unhook the first few trout without getting my hands wet by neatly tipping out the hook with a pair of forceps, but the next one took the fly deep in the roof of his mouth and I had to cradle him upside down in the current to remove it. Then I executed the practiced maneuver of tucking the rod above the left elbow with the hands in the armpits for warmth and looked around. It must have been about four-thirty in the afternoon, but the cloud ceiling was low and dense enough to obscure the lip of the canyon and dampen the light, so it looked more like seven. The two little summer cabins on the far bank were still shuttered and empty and there'd only been that one car on the sometimes well-traveled canyon road. The breeze probably hadn't picked up any, but the air was colder, and the snoosh had solidified into fine-grained corn snow that felt like wet sandpaper on my cheek. My nose was running uncontrollably.

The mystery of the empty river was beginning to

sort itself out, not to mention the sometimes fine distinction between bravery and stupidity. It was beginning to look as though no one was out there fishing for the obvious reason that it was just too damned cold to fish.

The idea of suffering for sport can seem noble before and after the fact, but at the actual moment you can begin to wonder just what the hell you're doing. I tried to feel sorry for my friend stuck in his meeting, imagining that he was uncomfortable in a different and worse way, but I knew that wouldn't be true. He's not a whiner or one to hold a grudge, so once he decided to work instead of fish, he'd simply swallow any regret, do his job and just generally take it like a man, as we used to say.

It *is* true that this guy is eagerly looking forward to retirement in less than two years and that if you woke him out of a sound sleep he could still tell you exactly how many days he has left. It's also true that when he retires he plans to teach fly casting, do some drift boat guiding and turn out more of the surprisingly good bamboo fly rods he's been building in his spare time, all of which will amount to a much better gig. His only real worry is that the pension and health care he's put in the last thirty years to get will be pulled out from under him, as it's been from so many others who made the mistake of believing the corporate promise.

He handles it all surprisingly well, although his high-pressure work environment and a chronic lack of sleep do sometimes cause him to be a little scattered. I've suggested that when he's finally finished with the job he should write a fishing memoir titled *Dude, Where's My Waders?*

Of course I have no such worries because as a freelance writer there was never a retirement package to lose, which can seem relatively unimportant when there's no urge to retire. Other advantages include either no boss at all or so many bosses you can afford to ignore the annoying ones, and no need to look busy when you're not. When you work for yourself, it soon becomes evident that you can't do everything, so the art becomes figuring out what to leave undone and why. That could explain all the fishing trips as well as the continuing absence of my Great American Novel. In the end, you pay roughly the same price for responsibility and recklessness, only in different currencies.

I guess I'm still trying to get used to the idea of my friends having real adult problems and responsibilities, even those who have become very successful through the usual avenues of hard work, long hours and pure native intelligence. I keep thinking that if you're a fisherman, any occupation that keeps you off the water should pay higher dividends than most of them do. It's not lost on me that if most people didn't do that, I wouldn't be able to do something as magnificently pointless as *this*; I just don't want to be standing next to any of them when their heads explode.

After five minutes of being tucked up in the classic cold fisherman pose, my hands were no warmer and I had one of those involuntary shivers that, along with morbid introspection, are among the first, still-reversible signs of hypothermia. I decided to catch one more trout for good measure and then pack it in. I'd already spotted a nice rainbow while I was standing there, so I paid out some line and made what I thought would be a slick, one-handed version of a snap-T spey cast. But it went wrong, as casts sometimes do, and I ended up with a complicated tangle involving my entire tippet, the fly, and the twist of lead weight. I retrieved this mess and examined it. Normally, I'd either carefully pick it apart or cut it off and retie the tippet, but my frozen fingers were all but useless and I was shivering a little too much for fine work, so there was nothing to do but trudge back to the truck. I put the rod, tangle and all, under the driver's side windshield wiper so I wouldn't forget and drive off without it. I considered getting out of my waders, but the laces on the wading shoes would present the same problem as the snarled leader.

It took some effort to get my key in the ignition without feeling in my hands, but I finally got the motor running and the heater blasting. There was some relief just getting into the cab and out of the wind, and more yet as the heater warmed up, but as my frozen fingers began to thaw they stung as if the tip of each one had been whacked with a ball-peen hammer. I couldn't help wondering what the stupid people were doing for fun that day.

19. The New Guy

Inviting Jim Babb along on the fall trip to the Fryingpan River was the most natural thing in the world. In one way or another he was known to all of us as an experienced fisherman, an all-around good guy and a compatriot: that is, some kind of misfit who, against the odds, had managed to pass for near normal out in the big world as the editor of a high-end sporting magazine. It also turns out that we're distant cousins— or what passes for cousins in Tennessee, where we both have family. (We figured this out while we were stranded together in a cabin in Canada for several days during a vicious storm and had long since run out of anything else to talk about.) And he was going to be in Denver for the Fly

Tackle Dealer Show anyway, so it was what they call a no-brainer.

I don't remember how many years ago it was that A.K., Ed Engle, Mike Clark and I started arranging this annual trip to coincide with the end of the Dealer Show, but I do remember that it was a little more than just a scheduling convenience. We all now end up going to the show for one reason or another and it's always worthwhile, but after a few days of exposure to the indoor, business end of the sport, the obvious antidote is a week of camping and actual fishing with friends.

Of course we're not the only ones to think of that, and in the weeks surrounding the show there are tackle industry types scattered all over Colorado's rivers, alone and in groups, with and without professional guides. Still, there *are* those lost souls who close the show and just go back to the office. They deserve our pity. Anyone who wouldn't stretch an expense-account plane ticket into a few days of fishing is bucking for a heart attack, and any company that wouldn't wink at that kind of shenanigan should just get out of the tackle business.

Before the trip Jim and I had the obligatory phone conversation about the fishing. He said he'd heard that the Pan was "difficult." I said the river's reputation was slightly exaggerated but that it did have its moments, admitting that even after more than thirty years there were still days when I'd find myself staring at rising trout while my skull slowly filled with a substance resembling damp steel wool. I said not to worry: that I'd seen him fish and knew he was up to it and that between us we'd have whatever specialized flies he'd need. We both understood that even on technical water, having the exact right fly is no more than 10 percent of the equation, but *believing* you have the right fly can bump it up to 15 or 20 percent.

Even as I said it, I remembered how I'd felt when I'd heard the same kind of thing in the past: "Sure, it can be tough, but a fisherman of your caliber won't have any trouble." No pressure or anything.

I shepherded Jim around for the first few days on the river—trying to be a good host even if I'm not much of a guide—but except for the loan of the occasional fly, he didn't need help. He fished with that unhurried smoothness some fishermen have: with no strain, no wasted motion and not much apparent effort. You might not point him out and say "That guy's good," but you'd notice that he was catching a lot of fish and you might wonder why.

Then, on the second day, he caught a large and difficult rainbow on a size 24 parachute Blue-winged Olive. It was a fish you might not have spotted in the first place—rising an inch from a rock in a backwater way over across the river—and then there was the long, accurate cast, the elaborate mend, the tricky drift and a set that would take up a lot of slack and come up just tight, without bending open the little hook or popping the fine tippet. Jim just sort of caught the fish and after that I stopped hovering.

The five of us were camped in our usual spot on the river at our friend Roy Palm's place, and the weather was on the wintry side of typical for fall, with a cold, steady daytime drizzle predictably turning to overnight snow and stiff, frosty mornings that would start when you chipped the ice off your tent as the first pot of coffee brewed. We lived in waders and rain gear to stay dry and kept a fire going in camp constantly, banking it up when we left to fish or turned in at night and then blowing it back to life from the coals. I honestly think we had three or four days' worth of fires off a single match.

The previous year in that same spot, the weather had been warmer and drier, but we'd had an awful windstorm that literally wrecked the camp. We'd all been upstream at the time, trying to fish tiny dry flies to bank risers in a hurricane-force gale. We'd noticed leaves and twigs going by in the current while we were fishing and as we drove back downstream to Roy's, there were larger limbs all but blocking the road in places. When we got back to camp, we found it in ruins. The tarp we'd stretched between trees as a rain fly had snapped most of its tie-downs and was shredded. So was the rain fly on Mike's pup tent. A.K.'s entire dome tent had been pulled up by the stakes and smashed against his pickup, irreparably twisting the aluminum poles. A lawn chair and a folding table were wadded up beyond recognition. A large cooking pot was missing (probably blown into the river and sunk) and an eighty-foot-tall narrow-leaf cottonwood had blown over, missing my parked pickup by no more than six inches.

Mike said, "Bummer," and that was the extent of the whining. The wind had died by then and there were a few trout rising in the camp pool, so we decided that cleaning up the mess could wait till later.

This year that tree was neatly bucked up into a cord of firewood and we burned a third of it to stay warm, proving once again that in the fullness of time, everything works out well enough, if not actually for the best. That is, in a cold week a year later, the windfall cottonwood seemed serendipitous, but of course for the price of the ruined gear that had to be replaced, we could have bought four times that much firewood.

You always subject the new guy to these pointless stories of past horrors and heroism. It's part of the normal drill: a polite alternative to marking the boundaries of your territory with urine. Of course in the long haul the river belongs only to God and the people, but the more years you have in on it the more of a claim you feel you have, so there's always a little bit of proprietary swaggering. The guest completes the ritual by pretending to be interested, if not actually impressed.

Still, fitting in is not always a foregone conclusion. We all know that these old, established gangs of fishermen can be like gated communities, or maybe halfway houses, complete with unspoken rules and walking wounded. They're all unique, but still weirdly similar. Maybe there are signs of past or even current substance abuse, or a residue of lost jobs, wives, houses, dogs or any of the other things you can lose over time, or a guy who still wakes up screaming from Vietnam nightmares. Maybe there's the quiet undertow of old differences that were dropped without being entirely settled, but dropped and all but forgotten nonetheless in favor of shared history.

This camaraderie extends far off the river, and that part of it is entirely genuine, although it's also somewhat residual. You could say that none of this is actually about the fishing and be pretty close to right. On the other hand, you could say it was *precisely* about the fishing and not be wrong. To all outward appearances, camp life involves little more than sitting in lawn chairs drinking coffee and talking, but the scene could not be successfully transplanted to a sidewalk café.

However it shakes out, you're always at a disadvantage as the new guy. You never quite know what to expect, there are inside jokes you won't get and you'll never know what subjects are taboo unless someone takes you aside and tells you—and no one ever does. What you get is a trip to a new river with people who know it pretty well. What you provide is your own novel approach to the fishing and some relief from years of conversational inbreeding. In the end, you'll do just fine if you help with the chores, don't complain and remember that fishermen have everything to learn from each other and nothing to prove. It helps if you're a good fisherman, but in all but the most competitive camps that part is optional.

Unless you're a total dim bulb, you'll also add something to the ongoing mythology of a regular camp. In addition to being a pretty good fisherman, Jim was an equally good camp cook, and as a former commercial fisherman, he knew all sorts of useful knots. He also added greatly to the usual free-form silliness. For instance, at Jim's instigation, we decided to start a rock band and call it Bad Haggis. For a brief moment it sounded like a decent idea, but then I remembered Grace Slick, formerly of the Jefferson Airplane, saying, "There's nothing sadder than watching old people try to play rock and roll."

That may or may not have been the night two field mice chewed a tennis-ball-sized hole in Jim's tent and woke him up by loudly attacking his supply of granola bars. Apparently this hadn't been much fun at the time, but over coffee the next morning he told it as a funny story. The picture of a grown man trying to herd two mice back through that little hole in the dark *was* pretty amusing, but I also knew from experience that when you wake from a sound sleep to find an uninvited animal in your tent, there's a horrifying moment when you don't know if it's a mouse, a skunk or a bear.

The official indoctrination speech finally came from Roy, who said to Jim one night, in his usual diplomatic way, "When I heard you were an editor from back East, I figured you'd be some Gucci-wearin', stuck-up motherfucker, but you're actually okay."

The hatches that week consisted of the usual suspects for the time of year and the bugs came off well in the cold, gray drizzle that both trout and mayflies like, never mind the discomfort of the fishermen. You desperately want your river to show off for a guest, and I beamed proudly every time we found rising fish, as if I had anything whatsoever to do with it.

I ran down the hatches for Jim, thinking it might be helpful. You know, the predominant bugs, the common masking hatches, the rare and sometimes important appearances and the odd stuff even an observant fisherman might miss, like the small yellow crane flies that are too easily mistaken for pale morning duns and the strange little saratella mayflies that always sound like the punch line to a bad joke in that they're said to be flightless, hermaphroditic and born pregnant.

I told Jim I could remember when the now-common sulphur mayflies were unknown on the Fryingpan. You never saw them and you never heard about them, even from the local hotshots who knew everything. Then one year they were big news—a new and heretofore unknown hatch—and within a few seasons, sulphur duns and spinners were standard equipment. Where did they come from?

At about that same time, the big mayfly known as a slate-winged drake began to vanish. This was a beautiful size 12 red quill that some said was a late-season, reddish-brown variation of the green drake and others claimed was a separate species altogether: the *Ephemerella coloradensis*. This was once an important autumn hatch with its own pattern—a standard green drake but with a maroon-dubbed body ribbed in pale green—but I haven't seen one in at least a dozen years. Where did they go?

Things like that can seem profoundly puzzling, but then Rudi Dam, the bottom-draw structure that turned the lower Fryingpan from a freestone to a tailwater, was built less than forty years ago and a fisheries biologist once told me it can take a century or more for a river to adjust to the changes in water temperature and chemistry. In the limited view of fishermen, things seem permanent here, but in truth the river is still figuring out what to do with itself and we're just along for the ride.

I also couldn't help but point out to Jim some luscious-looking stretches of river that you could once fish but can't now because they're posted. This seems to happen everywhere eventually. The old, laid-back landowners who used to let you fish their water move or die or get taxed into bankruptcy as property values increase, only to be replaced by wealthier, less generous types.

As always, one man's real estate deal is another man's swindle, and there can be hard feelings as old cabins bloom into mansions and NO FISHING signs sprout overnight like mushrooms. As Paul Gauguin once said, "Life being what it is, one dreams of revenge," and in recent years we've seen the development of "aerial poaching," or standing in public water and casting into private.

One afternoon between hatches, I even started in on how the fish used to be bigger here but lost steam after I saw Jim's skeptical glance. It does seem true, but then over the years we've drifted away from the shoulder-to-shoulder hog holes up under the dam (the most famous one is known as "the Toilet Bowl") into lesser, but also less crowded, water downstream that we've since come to know and love. And when I go back over old photos and see that the Fryingpan fish don't seem as big as I remember, it's not entirely reasonable to assume that all the snapshots of the really big trout must have gotten lost.

Jim listened to all this politely, understanding that the old-timer's litany we all grew up hearing becomes irresistible once you realize that the list of things that just aren't the same anymore will soon include you—if it doesn't already.

The new guy is a captive audience for this kind of grandstanding, but even as you drone on, you begin to envy the way he shrugs it off. He's fishing well, catching trout and looking at a new river with fresh eyes—seeing it just as it is instead of compared to how it used to be. More than once Jim said, simply enough, "This is beautiful," and he was right. It's my own little corner of what matters and I thought, How could life possibly go on without this?